The ESSENTIALS® of

Business Law II

William D. Keller, Ed.D.
Professor of Accounting
Ferris State University, Big Rapids, Michigan

> This book is a continuation of the "*THE ESSENTIALS OF BUSINESS LAW I*" and begins with Chapter 11. It covers the usual course outline of Business Law II. Earlier/basic topics are covered in "*THE ESSENTIALS OF BUSINESS LAW I.*"

Research & Education Association
61 Ethel Road West
Piscataway, New Jersey 08854

THE ESSENTIALS®
OF BUSINESS LAW II

Printed in the United States of America

Library of Congress Control Number 2003109204

International Standard Book Number 0-87891-729-2

ESSENTIALS is a registered trademark of Research & Education Association, Piscataway, New Jersey 08854

WHAT "THE ESSENTIALS" WILL DO FOR YOU

This book is a review and study guide. It is comprehensive and it is concise.

It helps in preparing for exams and in doing homework, and remains a handy reference source at all times.

It condenses the vast amount of detail characteristic of the subject matter and summarizes the **essentials** of the field.

It will thus save hours of study and preparation time.

The book provides quick access to the important principles, concepts, doctrines, and legal terms in the field.

Materials needed for exams can be reviewed in summary form— eliminating the need to read and re-read many pages of textbook and class notes. The summaries will even tend to bring detail to mind that had been previously read or noted.

This "ESSENTIALS" book has been prepared by an expert in the field, and has been carefully reviewed to ensure accuracy and maximum usefulness.

Dr. Max Fogiel
Program Director

CONTENTS

This book is a continuation of *"THE ESSENTIALS OF BUSINESS LAW I"* and begins with Chapter 11. It covers the usual course outline of BUSINESS LAW II. Earlier/basic topics are covered in *"THE ESSENTIALS OF BUSINESS LAW I."*

CHAPTER 11

COMMERCIAL PAPER

11.1 NEGOTIABLE INSTRUMENTS

Negotiable Instruments are writings drawn in a special form which can be transferred from person to person as a substitute for money or an instrument of credit.

EXAMPLE

Checks, Notes, and Drafts.

Rules For Negotiable Instruments are part of the Uniform Commercial Code which has been adopted by all the states.

Negotiation is transferring ownership of a negotiable instrument to another party by signing one's name on the back of the paper and by transferring the negotiable instrument to another person.

Order Paper is negotiated only by endorsement, by signing one's name on the back. On the face (front) of the paper it may say *Pay To The Order Of*.

Bearer Paper is a type of negotiable instrument that does not require endorsement (signing one's name on the back) for negotiation. Just the mere handing of the paper from one person to another is enough. On the front of the paper it may say *Pay To The Bearer*.

11.2 PROMISSORY NOTES AND DRAFTS

Types of Commercial Paper are promissory notes and drafts (and a check is a type of draft).

A draft (also called Bill of Exchange) is a written order, signed by one person, and requiring the person to whom it is addressed to pay on demand or at a particular time a sum certain in money to the order of a third person, or to the bearer.

A check is a type of draft where the drawee is the bank. Parties to a Check are:

1. **Payee** is the party who is to get the money.

2. **Drawer** is the party who writes and signs the check.

3. **Drawee** is the party who is ordered to pay the check. (The bank.)

Promissory Note is an unconditional promise in writing made by one person to another, signed by the maker engaging to pay on demand, or at a particular time, a sum certain in

$6,000.00	Big Rapids, Michigan	August 1, 2004

One year after date, for value received, I promise to pay to the order of James Brown the sum of $6,000.00 with interest thereon from date at the rate of 6% per annum, interest payable semi-annually, and if interest is not paid semiannually, to become as principal and bear the same rate of interest. Payable at FIRST NATIONAL BANK OF BIG RAPIDS, MICHIGAN

_____

(Signature of Maker)

money to order or bearer.

Parties to a Promissory Note are the Maker and the Payee.

— The Maker is the person who writes and signs the promissory note.

— The Payee is the person to whom the note is made; the one to receive the money.

Other parties to negotiable instruments are as follows:

— The Bearer is the person in possession of the negotiable instrument.

— The Holder is the person in possession where the paper has been made payable to this person's order.

— The Holder in Due Course is a Holder who takes a negotiable instrument in good faith and for value.

— The Indorser is the person who signs his or her name on the back of the negotiable instrument by an indorsement which names this person as the one to whom the instrument is negotiated.

— The Indorsee is a person who becomes the holder of a negotiable instrument by being named on the back of the instrument by the prior indorser.

11.3   REQUIREMENTS FOR NEGOTIABILITY

The instrument must be in writing and signed by the person negotiating it.

The instrument must contain either an *Order to Pay* or a *Promise to Pay*.

115

The order or promise must be *unconditional*.

The instrument must provide for the payment of a sum certain in money.

The instrument must be payable either on demand or at a fixed or definite time.

The instrument must be payable to the order of a payee or bearer.

The payee (unless the instrument is payable to bearer) and the drawee must be designated with reasonable certainty.

11.4   OTHER TYPES OF PROMISSORY NOTES

Bonds are written contracts, obligations generally issued by a corporation, a municipality, or a government, which contain a promise to pay a sum certain in money at a fixed or determinable future time.

— A Mortgage Bond is a type of bond which lists the asset or assets of the corporation that secure the bond (such as railroad cars or a railroad bridge). These would become the property of the bondholder in case of default on the bond of either principal or interest.

— A Debenture Bond is a bond that *does not list* any particular asset to be mortgaged in case of failure to pay the bond principal at maturity or failure to pay bond interest.

— A Coupon Bond is a type of bond having detachable individual coupons affixed to it, usually payable to bearer. The coupons are presented to the bank on the interest payment date, and the bank gives the bearer the interest money.

— A Registered Bond is a type of bond where the person who

owns the bond has his or her name on the face of the bond. Also, the name and address of the person owning the bond are listed on the books of the corporation issuing the bond. On each interest payment date the corporation or its representative mails a check to the registered bondholder. If the bond owner sells his or her bond to another person, the new owner's name and address must be placed on the books of the corporation and on the bond certificate.

Certificates of Deposit are acknowledgements by a bank of receipt of money with an engagement or promise to repay it. Normally the money is later repaid with interest. *Since a Certificate of Deposit does not contain the word "Promise," it is not negotiable.*

11.5 TYPES OF DRAFTS

Sight Drafts are drafts payable at sight or upon presentation by the payee or holder. The drawer demands payment at once.

EXAMPLE
Money Orders and Checks.

Time Drafts are similar to sight drafts except the drawee is ordered to pay the money a certain number of days or months after the date on the instrument or a certain number of days or months after presentation.

Trade Acceptances are a type of draft used in the selling of goods. They are drafts drawn by the seller on the purchaser of goods sold to and accepted by such purchasers. They are drawn at the time the goods are sold. The seller is the drawer, and the purchaser is the drawee.

Money Orders are instruments issued by banks, post offices, or express companies indicating that the payee may request and receive the amount indicated on the instrument. They are a safe way to send money by mail, because if the mail is lost or stolen, the sender will be able to recover the money from the firm that issued the money order.

11.6 TYPES OF CHECKS

Checks are a type of draft which is drawn on a bank and payable on demand. The bank is always the drawee. The drawer is always a depositor of the bank.

Certified Checks are ordinary checks which an official of the bank, the drawee, has accepted by writing across the face of the check the word *Certified,* and signed. It means that the check will not bounce.

Cashier's Checks are checks that a bank draws on its own funds and that are signed by the cashier or some other bank official. These checks may be used by a bank in paying its own debts, or they may be used by a bank customer who wishes to remit money in some form other than a personal check. It guarantees to the recipient of the check the full faith and credit of the bank issuing it.

A Voucher Check is a check with a voucher attached. The voucher lists the items of an invoice for which the check is a means of payment.

Traveler's Checks are instruments much like cashier's checks except that they require signature and counter-signature by the purchasers. They are sold by banks and express companies and are payable on demand. The purchaser of traveler's checks signs each check once at the time of purchase and then countersigns and fills in the name of the payee when the check is to be used. If a traveler's check is lost, the corporation issuing it will replace it, thus protecting the traveler's funds.

Postdated Checks are checks that are dated at a later date than written. (Let us assume that on July 1 we write a check but date it August 1. For the first month it is, in effect, a 31-day promissory note.) It is not illegal, but it is not payable until the date on the check.

Bad Checks are checks drawn by a bank customer who does not have enough money deposited in the bank to pay the amount of the check. *If a check is not made good within a specific period, such as ten days, there is a presumption of intent to defraud, and it becomes a crime.*

11.7 DUTIES OF THE BANK TO ITS DEPOSITORS

The Bank must maintain secrecy regarding information that the bank acquires in connection with the depositor-bank relationship.

If the bank pays a check which does not have the drawer's signature, the bank is liable to the drawer for the loss.

The bank must pay on demand all the depositors' checks to the extent of the funds deposited to their credit.

Stale Checks are those over 6 months old. The bank is not required to pay these.

11.8 STOPPING PAYMENT

Stopping Payment is a paid service of the bank to a depositor. After the depositor writes a check and gives it to the payee, the depositor who wrote the check can notify the bank not to pay it when it is presented for payment. This is useful when a check is lost or mislaid, or if a payee defaults on a contract. It, in effect, makes the check "bounce."

11.9 INDORSEMENTS

Indorsements are writings on the backs of checks or other negotiable instruments.

Blank Indorsements contain no words other than the signature of the indorser.

Special Indorsements designate the particular person to whom payment is to be made.

EXAMPLE

Pay To The Order of James Smith. William Jones.

Qualified Indorsements limit the liability of the endorser.

EXAMPLE

Pay to James Brown Without Recourse. Thomas Elliot. (This limits the indorser's liability; however, the indorser still warrants that the signatures on the instrument are genuine.)

The Liability of the Indorser is as follows: This person is secondarily liable; that is, (except for a qualified Indorser) the Indorser must pay if the primary party does not pay.

11.10 DISCHARGE OF OBLIGATION

Discharge of Obligation means the end of the obligation. Negotiable instruments may be discharged by *Payment, Renunciation, Alteration or Cancellation, Bankruptcy,* or *Lapse of Time.*

11.11 HOLDERS IN DUE COURSE

Holders in Due Course are innocent purchasers. To be a Holder in Due Course, a person:

1. Must take the instrument in good faith and for value.

2. Must have no notice that the instrument is overdue or has been dishonored.

3. Must have had no notice of any defense against or adverse claim to the instrument at the time the instrument is negotiated.

Holders through a Hold in Due Course are best explained by the example that follows.

EXAMPLE

Brown, a Holder in Due Course, transfers a note to Smith, but Smith did not give Brown any consideration. Therefore Smith is not a Holder in Due Course. However, Smith is a holder through a Holder in Due Course and thus derives all the protections from suit that Brown enjoys.

Defenses of a Holder in Due Course are strong and usually effective.

EXAMPLE

Let us say that the holder of commercial paper is not paid. This Holder in Due Course cannot get the money from the Drawee or Maker because that party is bankrupt. So the Holder in Due Course sues the previous holders who have their names signed on the back of the Commercial Paper. The Holder in Due Course is the Plaintiff and the Previous Holders are the Defendants.

The defenses of previous holders which cannot be raised against a Holder in Due Course are:

1. Ordinary contract defenses such as failure of consideration.

2. Fraud which induced the execution of the instrument: namely, false statements made at the time the instrument

was written.

3. Conditional Delivery.

EXAMPLE

Let us say the delivery boy was told not to deliver the instrument until a certain event happened, but he delivered it anyway.

4. Improper Completion — If any part of the commercial paper had originally been left blank, such as the name of the payee, or the amount, this cannot be held against a Holder in Due Course.

5. Payment or Part Payment — If payment has been made but the draft had not been turned over to the paying party, this cannot be used against a Holder in Due Course.

6. Nondelivery — This is best explained by the example that follows.

EXAMPLE

If one person makes out a Note to another person and that other person takes the Note from the maker's desk without the maker's permission and negotiates the Note to an innocent purchaser, or Holder in Due Course, the Holder in Due Course would be entitled to recover the amount of the Note against the maker.

7. Theft — Usually a thief cannot pass good title. However, a thief can pass good title to a Holder in Due Course.

Universal Defenses are defenses that can be raised against anybody, even against a Holder in Due Course. These are:

1. **Minority** — If a person is not of age, this person's contracts are meaningless as far as commercial paper is concerned.

2. **Forgery** — This is writing someone else's name on the commercial paper.

3. Fraud as to the Nature of the Instrument or its Material Terms.

EXAMPLE

An illiterate or a blind person signs a Note after having been falsely told it was something else.

4. **Bankruptcy** — If the maker has gone bankrupt, even a Holder in Due Course loses out.

Hybrid Defenses are valid in some courts but not in others. These are:

1. **Duress** — Force or threat of force in making out the paper.

2. **Incapacity** — The Signer is insane or feebleminded.

3. **Alteration** — A party to an instrument fraudulently makes a material (important) change in the commercial paper.

REVIEW QUESTIONS

1. What is a Negotiable Instrument?
A written or printed paper which can be transferred from person to person as a substitute for money.

2. If you can transfer the negotiable instrument to another person without signing it, what is it called?
Bearer Paper.

3. If you have to sign a negotiable instrument before you can transfer it to another person, what is it called?
Order Paper.

4. How does a draft differ from a check?
A check is a type of draft where the bank is the drawee.

5. How does a Draft differ from a Promissory Note?

A draft is written by the first party who orders a second party to pay a third party. A promissory note is written by the maker who promises to pay the second party, known as the payee.

6. Who is a Holder in Due Course?

A holder who takes a negotiable instrument in good faith and for value.

7. Who is an Indorser?

A person who signs his name on the back of a negotiable instrument.

8. Who is an Indorsee?

A person who becomes the holder of a negotiable instrument, he/she being named on the back of that instrument by the prior indorser.

9. How does a Bond differ from a Note?

A bond is usually for a longer period of time than a note — usually a bond is for 5 years or more — and a bond is usually issued by a government or a corporation.

10. How does a Mortgage Bond differ from a Debenture Bond?

A mortgage bond usually lists in the fine print on the face of the bond, a specific asset of the corporation which will be turned over to the bondholder in case the instrument is not paid at the due date. The debenture bond does not mortgage any specific assets of the corporation.

11. How does a Coupon Bond differ from a Registered Bond?

A coupon bond has interest coupons attached which can be separated from the bond at various interest dates, taken to the bank for the interest money. As a rule, coupon bonds are bearer bonds, and the names and addresses of the holders are not found on the books of the corporation or branch of government issuing them. On the other hand, registered bonds have the name of the owner printed on the bond and have the name and addresses of the bondholders printed on the books of the company. On every bond interest payment date the corporation or its agent sends a check to the bondholders.

12. How does a Certificate of Deposit differ from a Negotiable Instrument?

A Certificate of Deposit is not negotiable in the course of business from one person to another. A certificate of deposit is a bank acknowledgement that it has received money from a depositor, and that at the end of a certain period of time it will repay the depositor the amount invested plus a certain percent interest.

13. How does a Sight Draft differ from a Time Draft?

A Sight Draft is payable as soon as it is presented to the bank or to the party, and a Time Draft is payable on a certain date.

14. What is a Trade Acceptance?

It is a type of draft used in a sale.

15. Why do some people use money orders instead of their personal checks?

A personal check may bounce, but a money order is usually "as good as gold."

16. Who issues Money Orders?

Banks, post offices, and express companies.

17. How does a Certified Check differ from a Cashier's Check?

A certified check is a person's personal check where a bank official has written on it certified, followed by the official's signature. On the other hand, a cashier's check is the bank's check signed by a cashier. Both of these are methods of sending money by mail, where the recipient is assured that the check won't bounce. Certified checks and cashier's checks are also given in many other business transactions, including auctions, where the recipient has the benefit of knowing that they are as good as money and also knowing that if lost, they can be replaced.

18. How do Traveler's Checks differ from Cashier's Checks?

They both are guaranteed by the bank or express agency that issues them, but a person who uses a traveler's check must sign it twice — signing it the first time when buying the check, and countersigning it when cashing the check.

19. Are postdated checks legal?

Yes, unless there is fraud involved.

20. How does one write a postdated check?

One would write the date on the check as some date in the future. For example, let us suppose that this is January 2. We date the check February 2.

21. If a postdated check is written on January 2 and dated February 2, when can it be cashed?

On February 2 or thereafter.

22. What is a bad check?

One that bounces because the maker of the check does not have enough money in the bank to cover the amount of the check.

23. Is writing a bad check a crime?

Not if it is covered within ten days.

24. What is a stale check?

One that is cashed 6 months or more after it is dated.

25. How do you stop payment on a check?

By phoning or writing the bank giving them the number on the check, the date of the check, the amount of the check, and the name of the payee on the check, and telling them to stop payment.

26. Do most banks make a service charge for stopping payment on a check?

Yes. And it has grown larger in recent years.

27. Doesn't stopping payment on a check make it bounce?

Yes.

28. Can the maker of a stopped payment check be sued by the payee who did not get his money?

Yes.

29. What kind of indorsement is: "Pay to the Order of Mary Smith Without Recourse. Bill Smith"?

Special Indorsement.

30. If you write on the back of a check, "Pay to the Order of Mary Smith Without Recourse," what does that mean?

It is a Qualified Indorsement which limits the indorser's liability in case the bank does not pay.

31. What is a Holder in Due Course?

An innocent purchaser of the commercial paper.

32. What is a Holder through a Holder in Due Course?

A holder who has the commercial paper but did not give any money or any other consideration for it.

33. What are the rights of a Holder through a Holder in Due Course?

Usually the same as the rights of a Holder in Due Course.

34. A thief steals the commercial paper and passes it to a Holder in Due Course. Can the Holder in Due Course win a suit for the money from the maker of the commercial paper?

Yes.

35. The drawer of a check goes bankrupt. Can a Holder in Due Course get his money?

No, not from the drawer of the check, although he might try suing some of the indorsees.

CHAPTER 12

BAILMENTS

12.1 DEFINITION OF A BAILMENT

A Bailment is the transfer of possession, but not title, of personal property by one party, usually the owner, to another party on condition that the identical property will be returned or appropriately accounted for either to the owner or an agent at a future date or that it will be delivered to a person designated in the agreement.

The **Bailor** is the person who gives up possession.

The **Bailee** is the person who acquires possession but not title.

12.2 ORDINARY AND EXTRAORDINARY BAILMENTS

Extraordinary Bailments are those of Innkeepers and Common Carriers. The law imposes unusual liabilities on them.

Ordinary Bailments are all other bailments.

12.3 CONDITIONS OF A BAILMENT

The two conditions of a Bailment are:

1. Both parties agree that the same property is to be returned to the bailor or accounted for as directed. The property may be in greatly altered form. Also it could be understood that the bailee is to deliver the property to third persons or sell the item for the bailor.

2. There must be both **Delivery** and **Acceptance** of the property.

EXAMPLES OF BAILMENTS

A businessperson stores inventory in the warehouse of another.

A businessperson leaves his truck in a garage for repairs.

A person borrows a dress to wear to the dance.

A family leaves the dog with a friend while on a trip.

12.4   TYPES OF BAILMENTS

Express Bailment is a result of written or spoken words.

Implied Bailment is a result of actions (such as checking one's coat upon entering the theater).

12.5   DELIVERY AND ACCEPTANCE

Delivery and Acceptance are required in a bailment.

An example of Actual Delivery and Acceptance is: The garage (Defendant) actually gets temporary possession of Jim's (Plaintiff) car to be repaired.

Constructive Delivery and Acceptance is: Jim (Plaintiff) loses his billfold, and it is found by Mary (Defendant). This is Constructive Delivery and Acceptance. Jim is the bailor and Mary the bailee.

12.6   BAILMENTS FOR THE SOLE BENEFIT
OF THE BAILOR

Following is an example of a Bailment for the Sole Benefit of the Bailor: Bill (Plaintiff) asks John (Defendant) to keep his dog while Bill is on vacation. John gets no money for this. This type of bailee must exercise at least slight care and is liable only for gross negligence.

12.7   BAILMENTS FOR THE SOLE BENEFIT
OF THE BAILEE

Following is an example of a Bailment for the Sole Benefit of the Bailee: Harry (Defendant) borrows Jim's (Plaintiff) hunting dogs to go on a hunting trip and pays Jim nothing. Bailee (Harry) must exercise great care and is liable for even slight negligence.

12.8   BAILMENTS FOR MUTUAL BENEFIT

Following is an example of a Bailment for the Mutual Benefit of Both Parties. (This is the most usual type of Bailment.) A car is left at a garage to be repaired by a mechanic. Both parties benefit. The bailee (garage) must take reasonable care of the bailed property. The bailor (customer or client) must furnish safe property.

Duties of a Bailor are to inform the bailee of any known defects to the property.

Duties of a Bailee are to take reasonable care of the property in a Mutual Benefit Bailment. If the contract calls for the bailee to insure the property, the bailee must do so. If the bailee then does not insure the property and the property is damaged or destroyed, the bailee is liable.

How is an *Innocent Third Party* treated? The bailor may mislead an innocent third person into believing that the bailee owns the property. In this situation, the bailee may convey good title.

EXAMPLE

Horace (Bailor and Plaintiff) bought a typewriter from The Brown Office Equipment Company (Bailee and Defendant). Horace paid for the machine but asked the Brown Company to leave it on display until he could pick it up. The Brown Office Equipment Company sold the typewriter to Lacey. Lacey gets good title. However, the company is liable to Horace.

A *Pawn* is a Mutual Benefit Bailment where a person deposits tangible personal property as security for some debt. The person can later receive this personal property back by paying the pawnbroker the amount of the loan plus interest.

EXAMPLE

A person (Bailor) has no money. He goes to the pawn shop, (Bailee), leaves a watch which he owns, and borrows $100 on the watch.

A *Pledge* is a Mutual Benefit Bailment where a person deposits *Intangible* personal property as a security for some debt.

EXAMPLE

A person (Bailor) goes to the bank (Bailee) and leaves a stock certificate which he owns with the banker who then loans the person money and temporarily keeps the stock certificate as collateral.

12.9 PRIVATE AND COMMON CARRIERS

Private Carriers transport goods or services for a fee. They do not hold themselves out to the public to serve all who apply. There must be special arrangements made each time. (Example: Moving Vans.) These are Mutual Benefit Bailments so Private Carriers must use ordinary care.

Common Carriers undertake to transport goods or services for all who apply.

A **Consignor** is a person who ships goods by common carrier.

A **Consignee** is a person to whom the goods are shipped.

A **Bill of Lading** is the contract between consignor and carrier listing such items as date, terms of shipment, articles to be shipped, name of carrier, and names of consignor and consignee.

A **Common Carrier** may refuse service:

1. If it is a service for which the Common Carrier is not equipped.

EXAMPLE

Perhaps the railroad does not have enough oil cars on the train so it cannot load more oil.

2. If it does not take passengers.

EXAMPLE

A freight train.

3. It does not have to transport an invalid unless this person is accompanied by an attendant.

4. It does not have to transport persons intending to cause injury to the passengers or to the carrier.

5. It does not have to transport persons with contagious diseases.

6. It does not have to transport intoxicated persons.

The *Liability Standard* for *Common Carriers* is higher than that for Private Carriers. The *Common Carrier* is an *Insurer* of the safety of the Transported Goods.

Exceptions to this are:

1. *Acts of God* such as *Floods* and *Fires*.

2. Acts of a Public Authority, such as Public Officials seizing firearms carried on the train; or Public Officials seizing drugs carried on the train.

3. Inherent Nature of the Goods, such as Decay of Vegetables, or Death of Livestock on the freight train from Natural Causes.

4. Acts of the Shipper, such as Improper Packaging or Packing.

5. Acts of Public Enemy, such as Damage to goods from organized warfare or from border excursions of foreign bandits.

Common Carriers today are permitted to limit their losses by adding some clauses to the Bill of Lading form:

1. Carrier can *Limit its Loss* to a *Specified Sum* or a *Specified Percent* of the value of the goods.

2. Some states allow the carrier to limit its loss due to leakage, breakage, spoilage, and losses due to riots, strikes, mobs, and robbers.

3. The Carrier has only the liability of a *Mutual Benefit Bailee* for the *Storage of Goods Before or After Shipment.*

4. **Common Carriers of Persons have the:**

   — Right to prescribe the place and time for *Payment of Fares.*

   — Right to prescribe certain *Rules of Conduct* (such as removing *Intoxicated Persons* or certain people with *Communicable Diseases).*

   — Right to reserve certain seats and coaches for certain passengers (those in sleeper cars).

   The Liability of Common Carriers of Persons is:

   — *Ordinary Care* while passengers are in the station.

   — *Utmost or Extraordinary Care* while passengers are on board the bus, train, or airplane.

   — Reasonable accommodations and services such as water facilities, electricity, clean toilets. However, there is usually no guarantee that a passenger will have a seat in the absence of an *Express Reservation.*

   — *Extraordinary Care* to protect passengers but *Not An Insurer of Passengers.* Injuries to passengers by an employee or other passengers subjects the carrier to liability for damages, providing the passenger is not to blame.

   — *Liability for Baggage of Passengers* by Common Carriers is that of an *Insurer* for baggage that the passenger has checked with the carrier. Baggage retained in the possession of the traveler (carry-on luggage) requires only *Reasonable or Ordinary Care* by the carrier.

Straight Bills of Lading are Non-Negotiable. The goods must be delivered to the consignee named on the Bill of Lading.

Order Bills of Lading are Negotiable. The goods must be sent to the person holding the Bill of Lading, and the Bill of Lading must be surrendered to the shipper (railroad) at the time the railroad delivers the goods. Thus, the goods are delivered to the person holding the Bill of Lading (the final party in the negotiation), not necessarily to the original consignee.

12.10 HOTELKEEPERS

Hotelkeepers as Bailees must exercise *Extraordinary Care* over their guests' property.

A Hotelkeeper is one who regularly provides lodging to transients for a fee.

The Duties of a Hotelkeeper are to take *Special Care of their Guests and their property as follows:*

1. To serve all who apply. They cannot discriminate because of race, color, religion, or national origin. They may, however, turn away drunks, violent criminals, those not dressed according to code, or persons if all rooms are filled.

2. To provide fire escapes, set up signs showing locations of fire escapes, and to provide steel doors leading to stairways between floors.

3. To insure guests' checked-in property except for:

   — Acts of God.

   — Acts of a Public Enemy.

— Acts of a Public Authority.

— The Inherent Nature of the Property.

Most modern statutes relieve the hotelkeeper to some extent from *Extreme Liability* by *putting a Contract on the doors of guests' rooms and providing a vault or other safe place for guests to deposit valuables.*

The guest must be *Received* by the hotel or motel. (Usually the person signs in.) People coming to the hotel merely to eat are *Patrons,* not *Guests.* Visitors in the guests' rooms are not *Guests.* People living permanently in apartment houses are not *Guests.*

Hotelkeepers have a *Lien* (legal claim) to the *Baggage* of guests for the value of the services rendered. This does not mean that the hotelkeeper can in most states place a lien on the guest's car. If the hotelkeeper returns the property to the guest and the guest takes this property from the premises, the hotelkeeper cannot later get a lien on the luggage.

12.11 BOARDINGHOUSE KEEPERS

Boardinghouse Keepers as *Bailees* must exercise only *Ordinary Care.* They supply living accommodations to permanent boarders.

Boardinghouse Keepers today are usually owners of apartment houses.

Most states have given them a right to place a lien (legal claim) on property of boarders who do not pay their bills (apartment dwellers).

A boardinghouse keeper need not accept all who apply to become tenants.

12.12 CRIMES AGAINST HOTELS AND BOARDING-HOUSES

Crimes against Hotels and Boardinghouses by guests or patrons are:

1. Defrauding the hotel or boardinghouse by intentionally leaving without paying their bills.

2. Removing their property secretly.

REVIEW QUESTIONS

1. How does a Bailment differ from a Sale?
A bailment transfers possession not title. A sale transfers title to the property.

2. How does a Bailor differ from a Bailee?
The Bailor owns the property but gives up possession to the Bailee. The Bailee holds the property but does not own it.

3. How do Extraordinary Bailments differ from Ordinary Bailments?
Extraordinary bailments are those of innkeepers and common carriers that have unusual liabilities. Ordinary bailments are all other bailments which usually only have ordinary liability.

4. If a person leaves his car at a garage for repairs, is this a Bailment or a Sale?
Bailment.

5. If we check our hat with the hat-checker upon entering a hotel, and if we say nothing, is this an Express Bailment or an Implied Bailment?
An implied bailment.

**6. Mary asks Ann to keep her cat while Mary is on vacation. Ann gets no compensation for doing this. What kind of bailment is this?

Bailment for the Sole Benefit of the Bailor.

7. In Question 6 above, Ann feeds the cat but the cat runs away. Upon Mary's return from vacation, what happens?

Ann does not have to pay Mary anything, because under this Bailment for the Sole Benefit of the Bailor, the bailee need exercise only slight care, and this Ann did.

8. Harry borrows Jim's hunting dogs to go on a hunting trip and pays Jim nothing. While chasing a rabbit, one of the dogs runs off, never to be found. Will Harry have to pay Jim for losing one of his hunting dogs?

Yes. Harry is the bailee in a Bailment for the Sole Benefit of the Bailee and is bound to exercise great care.

9. Under what classification are most bailments?

Bailments for the Mutual Benefit of Both Parties.

10. What kind of care is required of the parties under a Bailment for the Mutual Benefit of Both Parties?

Reasonable Care.

11. A soldier runs out of money until payday. So he takes his watch to a store and leaves it there and borrows money from the store owner. What is he doing?

Pawning his watch.

12. In Question 11 above, how does the soldier get his watch back?

By paying the pawnbroker the amount of the loan plus interest.

13. How does a pawn differ from a pledge?

In a pawn, the borrower puts up tangible personal property such as a pocketwatch. In a pledge, the borrower puts up intangible personal property, such as a stock certificate.

14. How do Private Carriers differ from Common Carriers?

Common Carriers hold themselves out to any member of the public wishing to use their services. Private Carriers do not do this. Private Carriers can choose their customers.

15. How do the liabilities of Private Carriers differ from the liabilities of Common Carriers?

Private Carriers must exercise only Reasonable or Ordinary Care, while Common Carriers must exercise Extraordinary or Utmost care.

16. What is a Bill of Lading?

A contract between the consignor and the carrier.

17. What are some of the things listed in the Bill of Lading?

Date, terms of shipment, list of items to be shipped, name of the carrier, name of the consignor, name of the consignee.

18. Who is the Consignee?

The person to whom the goods are to be shipped.

19. In what situations may a common carrier refuse freight service?

If it is not equipped to carry a certain type of freight, or perhaps the railroad does not have enough oil cars available so it cannot load more oil.

20. Does the railroad have to take drunks, robbers, or people with contagious diseases?

No.

21. For what circumstances are common carriers not liable?

For Acts of God, Acts of a Public Authority, Inherent Nature of the Goods, Acts of Shipper, or Acts of a Public Enemy.

22. Are strikers considered public enemies?

No.

23. What are Acts of God?

Flood, fire, storm, earthquake.

24. How do Straight Bills of Lading differ from Order Bills of Lading?

Straight Bills of Lading are non-negotiable, and the shipper must deliver the goods to the consignee named on the Bill of Lading. On the other hand, Order Bills of Lading can be negotiated to third parties who then should receive the delivery from the carrier.

25. Can a railroad, bus company, or airplane company require that you buy a ticket before you board?

Yes.

26. What liability does a common carrier have as regards baggage?

It has to take extraordinary or utmost care of baggage checked with it. As for unchecked baggage, carry-on luggage, it has only ordinary or reasonable care required.

27. What type of care of passengers is required of the carrier while the passengers are in the station?

Ordinary or reasonable care.

28. What type of care of passengers is required of the carrier while the passengers are on the train, bus, boat, or airplane?

Extraordinary or utmost care.

29. How do Hotelkeepers differ from Boardinghouse Keepers?

Hotelkeepers regularly provide lodging to transients, while Boardinghouse Keepers have permanent tenants.

30. How do the liabilities of Hotelkeepers differ from the liabilities of Boardinghouse Keepers?

Hotelkeepers have extraordinary or utmost liability while boardinghouse keepers have only ordinary or reasonable liability.

31. Is the owner of a motel considered a hotelkeeper?

Yes.

32. Is the owner of an apartment house considered a boardinghouse keeper?

Yes.

33. Can hotelkeepers turn away people with contagious diseases?

Yes.

34. If a fire starts in a hotel through no fault of the owner, can the owner be successfully sued?

No.

35. If a person comes to a hotel for dinner, is he or she legally considered to be a guest?

No, he or she is a patron.

36. Are visitors in guests' rooms at a hotel or motel legally considered to be guests?

No.

37. Does a hotelkeeper legally have a lien on the baggage of guests who do not pay their bills?

Yes.

38. In an apartment house, does the owner have a lien on the property of renters who do not pay their bills?

Not under common law. But under the statutes of some states they now have this right.

CHAPTER 13

INSURANCE

13.1 PURPOSE OF INSURANCE

The Purpose of Insurance is to provide money when a loss covered by the policy is sustained. The policyholder makes a contract with an insurance company shifting to the insurance company the risk of financial loss.

13.2 INSURANCE TERMINOLOGY

Insurer is the insurance company.

Underwriter is another name for the insurance company.

The **Insured** is the policyholder.

The **Beneficiary** is the person who will receive the life insurance money upon the death of the insured.

The **Policy** is the Written Contract between the insured and insurer.

The **Face** is the amount of money the insurer agrees to pay.

The **Premium** is the amount of money the insured pays the insurer.

The **Hazards** are the factors against which the person may be insured, such as *Fire, Flood,* or *Hail.*

13.3 TYPES OF INSURANCE COMPANIES

Mutual Companies are companies owned by policyholders.

Stock Companies are companies owned by stockholders.

13.4 TERMS PECULIAR TO INSURANCE CONTRACTS

Concealment. This is willful and material hiding of some facts and will make an insurance contract void. The insured person must answer truthfully the questions asked by the insurance company at the time the policy is applied for.

Representation. False representation is putting down wrong information in answering the questions asked by the insurance company when a person is applying for a policy. Exception: Lying about a person's age does not invalidate the contract, but it does change the amount paid to the beneficiary.

Warranty. This is a statement of promise by the insured which appears in the contract.

Subrogation. This is the right of the insurance company to take the place of the insured.

EXAMPLE
The insured has a collision with the car of another party. If the insurance company pays the insured, then the insurance company has the right to sue the other party to the collision.

Estoppel. If one or the other party to an insurance contract violates the contract, in certain instances, the other party may not be able to benefit and may be **Stopped** from claiming this benefit.

EXAMPLE

The insurance company gives the insured a receipt for paying the insurance premium. Later the insurance company (the Plaintiff) claims it did not receive the premium money. The insurance company cannot get away with this assertion, as long as the insured (the Defendant) has the receipt of payment.

13.5   LIFE INSURANCE

Life Insurance is a contract wherein the Insurance Company promises to pay a sum of money to a beneficiary upon the death of the insured person.

Term Life Insurance is a type of life insurance which provides protection for a limited time stated in the policy. The cost is higher for each renewal period, because the insured is older and more likely to die. The amount to be received in case of death is either *Level* (for example $10,000 no matter when, in the term, the death occurs) or decreasing term (gradually less as the term progresses). There is no savings plan in a term insurance policy. It is pure protection and nothing more. The insured and the insured's beneficiaries get nothing unless the insured dies during the term of the policy.

Endowment Insurance is a type of life insurance which is a combination of a decreasing term insurance plus a savings account. Part of the premium pays for the insurance protection. The remainder is invested by the insurance company (this is the *Savings Feature* of the plan) and pays interest. At the end of the term, the total of the investment plus interest will equal the face amount of the policy. If the insured person dies during the term of the policy, the insured's beneficiary will collect the face amount of the policy. If the insured person is still alive at the end of the term, either the insured or the insured's beneficiary will collect the face amount of the policy, depending upon the wording of the policy. Endowment Insurance has some protection and a great deal of savings. Premiums on Endowment Insurance Policies (in relation to the face value) are much higher than are premiums on Term Life Insurance.

Whole Life Insurance is a policy that continues, assuming that premiums are consistently paid when due, until age 100 or death. If the insured is still alive at age 100, the company pays the insured the face value of the policy. If the insured dies before age 100, the company pays the beneficiary the face value of the policy. A whole life policy is a combination of protection and savings.

A Twenty-Pay Life Insurance Policy is one where the insured pays premiums for only the first 20 years. After this, the insured pays no more premiums. If the insured lives to age 100, the company pays the insured the face value of the policy. If the insured dies before age 100, the company pays the beneficiary the face value of the policy. The Twenty-Pay Life Insurance Policy (in relation to the face value) has higher premiums than has the Whole Life Insurance Policy.

Thirty-Pay Life Insurance Policy is one where the insured pays premiums for only the first 30 years. After this, the insured pays no more premiums. The Thirty-Pay Life Insurance Policy (in relation to the face value) has higher yearly premiums than does the Whole Life Insurance Policy but it has lower yearly premiums than does the Twenty-Pay Life Insurance Policy. If the insured lives to age 100, the company pays the insured the face value of the policy. If the insured dies before age 100, the company pays the insured's beneficiary the face value of the policy.

A Rider is a clause or a whole contract added to another contract to change the basic contract. The Disability Income Rider pays an income to the insured who becomes disabled. Naturally, when this rider is added to the policy, the premiums would become higher. Waiver of Premium Rider states that a disabled person who is insured no longer has to pay premiums, and his policy is still in force. In a Double Indemnity Rider, the insured pays a higher premium, so in case of accidental death of the insured, the company pays the beneficiary twice as much as the face value of the policy.

Annuities insure people from outliving their incomes. Money is given the insurance company when a person retires, usually at age 65, or premiums may be paid to the company at stated intervals prior to this time. The insurance company invests this money and each month, or quarterly, or annually, depending on the contract, pays the insured a check which covers the interest income plus part of the principal. This continues until the death of the insured. Joint and Survivor Annuities are agreements continuing payment by the company to the annuitant or annuitants until the second annuitant (usually the surviving spouse) dies. No medical exam is required of a person when buying an annuity.

Suicide Clauses are found in many life insurance policies. Most policies state they will not pay if a person commits suicide within two years after taking out the policy. They do pay if the suicide takes place after the two years.

War Clauses are found in some life insurance policies. These usually state that if the insured dies in a war, the company will not pay. However, if a member of the armed forces dies of natural causes, the company must pay.

Payment of Premiums is essential. In most cases a policy lapses if premiums are not paid on time, unless there is a

Waiver of Premiums clause. This clause states that the insured need not pay premiums during the time when the insured is disabled. Naturally, this type of policy is more expensive.

A Grace Period is required by law to be in all life insurance policies. This gives the insured a month extra beyond the regular date to pay the premiums before the policy lapses.

Incontestability means that after a year or two (depending on state law or premium wording) the insurance company cannot cancel the policy for any reason except for nonpayment of premiums.

Insurable Interest is necessary in life insurance. Examples of an insurable interest are: parents and children, husband and wife, partner and copartner, and a creditor in the life of the debtor to the extent of the debt. Insurable interest must exist at the time the policy is purchased, not necessarily at the time of the death of the insured. One person cannot take out insurance on the life of another person unless that person has an insurable interest in the person.

If this were not so, a person could take out an insurance policy on the life of an enemy and have him killed for the insurance.

A Change of Beneficiary is allowed. The insured in a life insurance policy can change the beneficiary at any time desired. This includes a policy where the beneficiary has been paying the premiums.

Assignment of a Policy by the insured is a possibility. An insured person may assign to someone else the value of the policy. The insured might do this by assigning the policy to the bank when borrowing money from the bank.

Borrowing money on a life policy is possible, except on Term Life policies. Usually the policy states how much may be borrowed by the insured and at what rate. The amount to be borrowed is usually the savings portion of the policy. The amount borrowed need never be paid back; but in that case it would lower the value to be paid the beneficiary on the death of the insured. Usually the interest rates are much lower on insurance policies than on other loans.

13.6   FIRE INSURANCE

Fire Insurance covers only the loss from the fire. So there is no use in insuring a building for more than it is worth. One would only pay higher premiums.

Flame is essential to a fire insurance policy. There must be flame to have a fire. Smoke or scorching loss are not covered.

A Hostile Fire is necessary. This is one out of its normal place. Smoke destruction from a friendly fire in a fireplace is not covered.

Economic loss while rebuilding is not covered by Fire Insurance. For this, one must be covered by Business Interruption Insurance.

Extended Coverage on a Fire Insurance Policy might cover windstorm, explosion, smoke, falling aircraft, riot, water damage, etc.

Insurable Interest is necessary both at the time one takes out the policy and at the time of the damage.

EXAMPLE

Examples of persons with insurable interest in a building: Owner, Mortgagee, Bailee, Partner, Tenant.

In an Open Policy the insured must prove how much was actually lost.

In a Valued Policy, each item will have a stated value in the policy. After a fire, no appraisal would be needed.

A Specific Policy is on one item only, such as a house.

A Blanket Policy is on many items of the same kind in different places, or of different kinds of property in the same place.

A Floating Policy covers the loss no matter where the property is located at the time of loss.

A Reporting Form for Merchandise Inventory is filled out when a merchant reports to the insurance company once a month the amount of inventory on hand. Then this amount is insured for the month.

Risk or Hazard minimization is important. When fire occurs, the insured must do everything possible to keep the amount of loss down.

80% Coinsurance Clauses mean that the insured must carry insurance worth at least 80% of the value of the property in order for the insurance company to pay the full amount of a partial loss.

EXAMPLE

We own a building worth $100,000 but have a fire insurance policy for only $40,000. There is an 80% Coinsurance Clause, which means that the owner will have to be part insurer and the company part insurer. (80% of $100,000 = $80,000.) The insurance of $40,000 is only half of the $80,000, so the company will never in this case pay more than half the damage and never will pay more than the $40,000, even in case of total destruction.

Cancellation of a policy is a possibility. The policy may be cancelled by either the insured or the insurer. If the insurer cancels, (the insurer being the Company), the company must repay the insured the amount of unearned premiums at the short-term rate.

13.7   AUTO INSURANCE

Auto Insurance is necessary for almost every driver.

Fire Insurance for an Auto covers a car that burns. It can be purchased separately but usually is part of comprehensive coverage.

Theft Insurance covers stealing the car and any parts of the car but not articles or clothes left in the car. It covers car damage during the theft.

Collision Insurance covers cars hitting other cars, rocks hitting cars, and such things as horses hitting cars. Deductible Clauses in policies help reduce premiums. This means that the Insurance Company pays part and the insured must pay the rest. There are policies without a Deductible Clause. In the case of an accident the Insurance Company must pay all the damages. But these policies have terribly high premiums.

Comprehensive Coverage covers only the hazards listed in the policy and does not usually cover Collision.

EXAMPLE

Flood, Earthquake, Windstorm, Strike, Mischief, Submersion in Water, Riot, Hail, etc.

In Bodily Injury Insurance the company promises to pay any amount, not exceeding the limit fixed in the policy for which the insured is personally liable, plus defending the insured in court actions brought by the injured persons.

EXAMPLE

25/50/10 means that the insurance company will pay up to $25,000 to any one person for bodily injury in any one accident. The company will pay up to $50,000 total to more than one person hurt in any one accident. The Company will pay $10,000 maximum for property damage in any one accident (usually damage to the other person's car.) Often policies will not pay if a car is operated by a person under driving age or if the car is being operated outside the United States or Canada.

Medical Payment Insurance pays medical bills of the insured or of passengers in the insured person's car.

Uninsured Motorist Insurance protects the insured when the insured's car is hit by the car of an uninsured motorist.

Notice to the Insurer is essential. After an accident, the insured must give the fullest cooperation to the insurance company.

EXAMPLE

The insured should give the insurance company the time, place, and circumstances of the accident, names and addresses of the injured persons, and owners of damaged property, and witnesses' names and addresses.

Last Clear Chance Rule is in effect in most states. If one driver is negligent, but the other driver had the last clear chance to avoid hitting the negligent driver and did not take it, then the driver who had the last clear chance is liable.

What are **Comparative Negligence Laws?** If both parties to the accident were negligent, the negligence of each party is balanced against that of the other to determine the amount of the damages.

151

No-Fault Insurance is now in effect in some states. The insurance companies pay for the injuries of their clients no matter who is at fault.

Financial Responsibility Laws are in effect in some states. Drivers are not required to have liability insurance until their first accident. If a person after the first accident cannot pay the claims, that person must take out a certain amount of liability insurance as stated in the state law.

The Assigned Risk Rule works as follows: If no insurance company will sell liability insurance to a driver, then the state insurance commissioner will assign this driver to an insurance company who must then sell him a policy.

13.8   SECURITY DEVICES

Security Devices are methods of getting others to pay your debts.

Contract of Guaranty (or Surety) is one where one person promises to pay the debt of another.

EXAMPLE

James Brown (the Principal) is age 18 and has no credit. He wants to borrow $5,000 from a local bank in order to buy a car. The bank insists on a surety. So James asks his uncle, Bill Smith, to become his surety. Bill Smith has good credit and a good job. Smith signs a statement at the bank that if James Brown does not pay the note and interest when due, that he (Bill Smith) will pay.

Fidelity Bond is a contract of surety, usually purchased through an insurance company, that guarantees that a person handling valuable money or property is covered.

The **Surety** has a primary liability, the same as the principal debtor. If the debtor will not pay, the surety must pay immediately.

A **Guaranty** is secondary liability only. The Guarantor must pay only if the principal debtor defaults.

Contracts of Surety may be either written or oral. Guaranty contracts must be written.

Notice of Default need not be given in suretyship but must be given in guaranteeship.

Rights of surety and guarantor are as follows:

1. **Indemnity** — If surety or guarantor pays the debt, that person has the right to be refunded by the principal.

2. **Subrogation** — The best explanation here is an illustration:

EXAMPLE

Brown (the Principal), wants to borrow $10,000 from the bank. Brown puts up his truck worth $2,000 and the bank files the truck's title in its vault. The bank asks that Brown produce a surety. Smith becomes surety for Brown's loan. Later Brown does not pay the loan to the bank, so Smith pays the loan. Smith then requests and obtains title to Brown's truck from the bank.

Contribution

EXAMPLE

Brown borrows $10,000 from the bank, with Harold and Smith as co-guarantors. Brown runs to Mexico, never to be seen again. Harold repays the bank its $10,000. Contribution is the right of co-guarantor Harold to collect the proportionate share (in this case $5,000) from Smith.

Exoneration

EXAMPLE

Brown borrows $10,000 from the bank, with Harold and Smith as co-guarantors. Brown's business continues to deteriorate and it looks as if he soon may go bankrupt. The bank takes its time attempting to get the $10,000 from Brown since it knows that the two guarantors are standing behind Brown. Exoneration is the right of the guarantors to call upon the bank to collect the debt immediately. If the bank fails to do this, the guarantors can be released from their potential liability through exoneration.

Other Methods by which a surety or guarantor may be released from promise:

1. **Extension of time** — If the bank (creditor) extends the time that the debt runs, without the consent of the surety, the surety or guarantor is relieved, as long as there is additional consideration.

2. **Alteration of the Contract's Terms** — If the creditor and debtor greatly (materially) change the terms of the contract, they have, in effect, started a new contract. This releases the surety or guarantor from liability.

3. Loss or Return of Collateral by the Creditor.

EXAMPLE

Brown borrowed $10,000 from the bank and the bank held title to Brown's $2,000 truck. Smith also became surety for the debt. Later the bank returned Brown's title papers on the truck to Brown. This released Smith's liability as surety.

Bonding Companies make agreements with businesses. Businesses pay premiums to bonding companies. Then if employees of the business run off with business funds, the bonding company must pay the business the amount of loss.

Secured Credit Sales occur when the buyer purchases goods on credit. If the buyer cannot pay for them, the seller has the right to repossess them.

Security agreement is a written agreement, signed by the buyer, describing the purchase, gives the names of the buyer and seller, and contains the terms of payment.

Default is failure of the buyer to pay for the goods.

Repossession is the right of the seller to repossess the goods after default. If buyer objects, the case may have to go through court.

After repossessing the goods, the seller may sell them to someone else (resale).

After repossession but before resale, the buyer may repossess his goods by paying the full price to the seller, plus any extra expenses and legal fees. This is termed redemption.

Seller and buyer must keep records and account to each other for expenses, and settle surplus or deficiency (accounting).

REVIEW QUESTIONS

1. Can all risks in life be insured?
No, only legal financial risks. For instance, we can insure the life of a loved one but cannot insure the life of an enemy.

2. Who owns a mutual insurance company?
The customers — that is, the policyholders.

3. The insured drives his car and has a collision through no fault of his own. The insurance company pays the insured. What is the name of the right of the insurance

company to get money from the other party to the collision?

Subrogation.

4. What type of life insurance is all protection and no savings?

Term Life Insurance.

5. Which type of insurance has a lower premium — level payment term, or decreasing payment term?

Decreasing payment term, because in all likelihood the company will pay less to the insured, unless the insured dies almost immediately after having taken out the policy.

6. If we buy a decreasing term policy that includes a savings account, what type of insurance is this?

Endowment.

7. How do premiums on an endowment policy compare to premiums on a term policy, in relation to the amount of insurance carried?

Endowment policy premiums are much higher.

8. Why are endowment policy premiums much higher than term policy premiums?

If a person does not die during the term of the policy, the term policy has no value at the end of the term, while the endowment policy has the entire value of the savings.

9. Why do some financial managers favor term insurance over endowment insurance?

Insurance is the only method of getting financial protection in case of death. But there are many other more profitable ways of investing savings than putting them into insurance policies.

10. How do endowment policies differ from whole life policies?

If a person does not die, the whole life policies pay off at age 100, but an endowment policy pays off at the end of what is usually a shorter term.

11. All else being equal, are premiums lower on a whole life policy or on an endowment policy?
Whole life policy.

12. What is a 20-pay life policy?
An insurance policy wherein the insured pays for only the first 20 years that the policy runs. After this, he is not repaid by the insurance company until he dies or reaches age 100.

13. Which has cheaper yearly premiums, the Whole Life Policy or the 20-year-pay policy?
Whole Life Policy.

14. Which has lower yearly premiums — the 20-pay-life policy or the 30-pay-life policy?
The 30-pay-life policy.

15. How does a Disability Income Rider affect the premiums on an insurance policy?
It increases the premium.

16. What types of plans insure people from outliving their incomes?
Annuity contracts.

17. What is a joint and survivor's annuity?
An annuity that continues paying until the surviving spouse dies.

18. What is a Grace Period?
The 30-day or 31-day time that the insured is allowed to pay the premium late without having the policy lapse.

19. What is Insurable Interest?
A close family relationship or a financial interest in the life of the insured.

20. In a Life Insurance Policy when does there have to be an insurable interest?

At the time the policy is purchased; not necessarily at the time of death.

21. When can the insured change the beneficiary on the insured's life insurance policy?

At any time.

22. When the insured borrows money from a bank, can he assign to the bank any benefits of the policy?

Yes.

23. Can a person borrow money on a term life insurance policy?

Not usually.

24. Why can a person not borrow on a term life insurance policy?

Money is borrowed on a life insurance policy from the savings portion of the policy; and a term policy has no savings feature, as a rule.

25. When in need of money, why is it a good idea to borrow on your insurance policy?

The amount borrowed need never be paid back, and usually the interest rate for borrowing on insurance policies is lower than the interest rates banks charge on loans.

26. Is it a good idea to insure your building for more than it is worth?

No, because in case of total destruction of the building by fire, the insurance company will only reimburse the insured the amount that the building is worth.

27. What is the difference between a hostile fire and a friendly fire?

A friendly fire is one in the fireplace, and a hostile fire is one that is burning down the house.

28. Does a fire insurance policy cover destruction by smoke?

Not unless there is a clause covering smoke. There must be flames before there is a fire.

29. Does a fire insurance policy cover economic loss that a business suffers from failure to do business after the building is burned down?

No, one must take out Business Interruption Insurance to cover this.

30. What is meant by Insurable Interest in a fire insurance policy?

Owner of the building, renter of the building, mortgage holder of the building.

31. In order to receive payment from a fire insurance company, when must a person have insurable interest in the building?

Both at the time the policy is purchased, and also at the time of the fire.

32. What is the name of a policy that covers loss no matter where the property is located at the time of loss?

Floating Policy.

33. What is meant by coinsurance?

The insurance company pays part of the loss and the insured pays part of the loss.

34. In a fire insurance policy, how long do the parties have to cancel?

Either party may cancel at any time; however, if the insurance company cancels, it must pay the insured the portion of unearned premiums at the short-term rate.

35. Why are there usually deductible clauses on collision insurance?

If there were none, the premiums would be exorbitantly high.

36. Who pays for an accident in no-fault insurance states?

The insurance company pays the claims of its own clients.

37. How can a person having had many accidents buy auto insurance?

Some states have an Assigned Risk Rule, whereby the State Insurance Commissioner forces various insurance companies to sell policies to these persons.

38. How does a surety differ from a guarantor?

A surety has primary liability in case of default, whereas a guarantor has only secondary liability.

CHAPTER 14

REAL PROPERTY

14.1 DEFINITION OF REAL PROPERTY

Real Property is land, buildings, fences, walls, timber, waters, and minerals under the soil. Thus, Real Property is land and anything attached to land, including clovers, grasses, and perennials.

A **Navigable River** is one deep and wide enough to provide for the passage of ships. On *Non-Navigable Rivers* the property owner owns the river bed but not the flowing water. The owner cannot impound the water. On Navigable Rivers the owner owns the land only to the low-water mark.

14.2 FIXTURES

Fixtures are personal property that have become real property. Personal property attached to land or building becomes real property if it is attached so securely that it cannot be removed without damaging the real property to which it is attached.

EXAMPLE

Probably curtains are personal property, but shades that have been attached to the window frame securely could be considered real property.

Was the affixing of the fixture to make it permanent? If it was installed for a permanent purpose, it becomes real property.

Who installed the fixture? If the **Landlord** installed the fixture, it is real property. If the **Tenant** installed the fixture, it remains personal property.

14.3 PERSONAL PROPERTY

Personal Property is any property that is not real property.

Tangible Personal Property is property that can be touched, such as: animals, furniture, merchandise, annual growing crops, jewelry.

Intangible Personal Property is property that cannot be touched. The Intangible Personal Property has evidences of ownership that can be touched — such as certificates. Examples of Intangible Personal Property are: copyrights, savings account certificates, stock certificates, bond certificates, checks, contracts, patent certificates, etc.

14.4 TYPES OF PROPERTY OWNERSHIP

A **Fee Simple Estate** is the highest ownership. This type of ownership gives the owner the right to possess the property forever (unless taken away by the State through Eminent Domain). The Fee Simple owner may sell the property or bequeath it.

In a **Life Estate** the owner has the right to use the property for the owner's lifetime but cannot sell or bequeath it. At the owner's death, the property either reverts to the grantor or goes to a person called *Remainder,* depending on the terms of the life estate.

14.5 METHODS OF ACQUIRING PROPERTY OWNERSHIP

Purchase.

Will — A beneficiary of another's will gains title to the property.

Gift — This is a legal transfer without consideration. (The recipient is not required to do anything.)

Descent — When a person dies intestate (without leaving a will), that person's property is disposed of according to the *Law of Descent* in that state.

Accession — The materials owned by two people are combined to form one product. The person who owned the major part of the materials then owns the product. Also it means title to future animal offspring.

Accretion — This is land acquired by the gradual deposit by water of solids (land washing up on a river bank or lake bank or ocean beach).

Confusion — This is the mixing of goods of different owners, such as lumber, oil, coal, or grain.

— If *Confusion* is brought on by *Common Consent* of the owners or by accident, each owner gets a proportionate part.

— If *Confusion* is brought on by willful act, the innocent party gets the whole property.

Creation is the producing of a new invention such as a play, piece of music, book, etc.

Inventions such as new cars or new mousetraps are protected by *Patents* through the U.S. Patent Office, allowing the inventor a number of years of exclusive use.

Written Items, such as musical compositions, paintings, architectural plans, books and magazine articles are protected by *Copyrights,* given by the Library of Congress, allowing the writer a number of years of exclusive use.

In **Adverse Possession** (squatter's rights) one must occupy the land continuously, openly, visibly, and exclusively for between seven and 21 years, depending on the state.

14.6 LOST PROPERTY

To become *Lost Property,* the owner must unintentionally leave the property somewhere. The finder of lost property has the right to possession against all but the true owner.

14.7 ABANDONED PROPERTY

Abandoned Property is actually discarded by the owner. The person who discovers this property owns it.

14.8 ENVIRONMENTAL LAW

Environmental Law concerns Air Pollution, Water Pollution, Solid Waste Disposal, Strip Mining, etc.

Major Legislation passed recently concerning environment is the Water Pollution Control Act, Clean Air Act, National Environmental Policy Act.

State Legislation has been passed by most states to regulate the environment. Some states have also set up agencies to enforce these laws.

14.9 TRANSFER OF REAL PROPERTY

Transfer of Real Property is effected by Deeds which are writings signed by the seller conveying title to real property.

Quitclaim Deeds are a type of deed in which the grantor gives up any claim to the property that the grantor may have had. The grantor does not warrant (guarantee) that he or she has any claim.

In **Warranty Deeds**, the grantor not only gives up claim to property but also makes a guarantee.

A **General Warranty Deed** guarantees no title defects. The Grantor has good title to the property. The Grantee is given quiet and peaceable possession free from encumbrances (mortgages).

A **Special Warranty Deed** warrants that the grantor has the right to sell the real property. This is used by sheriffs, trustees, and administrators. It does not guarantee against encumbrances (claims on property such as mortgages).

A deed will mention the following characteristics:

1. **Parties** — It gives the grantor's name and the grantee's name as well as the names of their spouses, if either are married.

2. **Consideration** — A Statement of Consideration must be made in the deed, but the amount specified in the deed need not be the actual amount paid.

3. **Covenants** — These are agreements specified in the deed.

EXAMPLES

An agreement to maintain a common driveway along with the owner of the adjoining property. An agreement not to use the property for business purposes.

4. **Signature** — A deed must be signed by the grantor and the spouse of grantor.

5. **Acknowledgment** — The Deed must be signed and stamped by a notary public and recorded at the courthouse. This protects the grantee from having the grantor later sell the property to someone else.

6. **Delivery** — The deed itself must be given to the grantee or to the grantee's attorney.

7. **Abstract of Title** — This is a history of the property and must be brought up to date by an Abstract Company or by an attorney. It also shows any unpaid taxes, assessments, and mortgages.

8. **Title Insurance** — If the new owner wishes to buy this, the new owner pays one premium to an insurance company which then guarantees the owner that no one will in the future come and obtain a better title through some earlier error.

14.10 MORTGAGES ON REAL ESTATE

Mortgages on Real Estate are liens based on real estate (land, buildings) in order to secure a debt. In a mortgage payment, unless otherwise stated, interest is paid first, then principal.

The **Mortgager** is the owner who puts up the property to secure a loan.

The **Mortgagee** is the person who holds the mortgage.

Default is failure to make mortgage payments on time.

Foreclosure Sale occurs after default, when the mortgagee takes over the property and sells it. If the mortgagee receives more than the debt and costs, that person turns over the remainder to the mortgager.

Mortgages must be in writing and should be recorded at the courthouse in order to protect both parties from adverse claims.

The **First Mortgage** must be paid off before other mortgages are considered. The First Mortgage is safer than are second or third mortgages on the same property.

14.11 DUTIES OF A MORTGAGER

Mortgager must pay interest and principal payments as they come due, depending on the wording of the mortgage.

Mortgager must pay taxes and any property assessments on the mortgaged property.

Mortgager cannot do an act that would hurt the security of the mortgagee, such as *Tear Down the Building,* or *Cut the Trees.*

14.12 RIGHTS OF THE MORTGAGER

Possession of the Property — The Mortgager may use the property and live on it.

Rents and Profits — Unless otherwise stated in the contract, the mortgager has the rights to the rents and profits from the property.

Cancellation of the Lien — When the mortgager makes the final payment on the mortgage, the mortgagee must go to the clerk's office and have the clerk make an entry certifying that the mortgage debt has been paid.

Redemption — During a specific time after foreclosure and sale, the mortgager may still get the property back by paying the amount of the mortgage and the costs of the sale.

14.13 FORECLOSURE

Foreclosure is a legal procedure where an officer of the court sells the mortgaged property.

Prior claims to the property are: Cost of Foreclosure, Taxes, Materials Furnishers' Bills, Mechanics' Liens. These must be paid from the proceeds of the foreclosure sale.

Any surplus from the sale must be returned to the Mortgager.

If the sale results in a deficiency, a court judgment will be made against the mortgager for the balance of the debt.

14.14 TRUST DEED

A **Trust Deed** is similar to a mortgage. It conveys title to a disinterested third party, a *Trustee*, who manages the property for the creditors.

14.15 BUYING MORTGAGED PROPERTY

Buying Mortgaged Property can be done in two ways:

1. **Assuming the Mortgage** — This is taking over the previous mortgage. The person who assumes the mortgage is primarily liable for its payment.

2. **Buying Property Subject to the Mortgage.** Here the buyer of the mortgaged property loses only what he or she has in the property, and no more. If the purchaser does **not** assume the mortgage but simply takes the property "subject to" the mortgage, the purchaser is **not** personally liable for the mortgage, nor is he or she a surety for the mortgage obligation. In this case the purchaser's exposure to loss is limited to the value of the property. Although the mortgagee creditor may foreclose against the property, he or she may not hold the purchaser personally liable for the debt.

14.16 LANDLORD AND TENANT

Landlord and Tenant Law concerns one person leasing land or a building to another. (A Lease is a long-term rent.)

Lease agreements for over a year must be in writing to be enforceable.

A **Tenant** has exclusive legal possession of the property.

A **Lodger** has the right to use the building, or part of the building under the supervision of the owner.

The **Lease** should be in writing to avoid disputes. It should mention which property is being leased, the names of the parties, the amount of rent, the time and place of payment of rent, the type of tenancy, and whether or not the landlord can show the property and redecorate the property.

Tenancy for Years is for a definite period of time. The ending date is mentioned in the lease.

Tenancy From Year to Year is a lease for an indefinite time. (If the rent is paid by the month, it is often called a *Tenancy From Month to Month.)*

Tenancy at Will is for an uncertain period. Either the tenant or the landlord can end this type of tenancy.

Tenancy at Sufferance is at the landlord's discretion. After the date of tenancy ends and the tenant does not leave, the law considers the stay a Tenancy of Sufferance. The landlord may either throw the tenant off the land and sue the tenant for the extra stay, or the landlord may let the tenant remain and charge the tenant rent.

Rights of the Tenant are:

1. **Right of Possession** — The Landlord must turn over the property in good shape to the tenant, and the landlord needs to agree to keep other tenants from disorderly conduct.

2. **Right to Use the Premises** — Tenant can use the premises for the purposes agreed on, but not for other purposes. (For instance, the Tenant may not use a private home for a factory.)

3. **Right to Assign or Sublease.** *Assignment* is when the tenant assigns the lease to someone else; to the Assignee, who then uses the property. The Assignee pays the rent directly to the landlord. This is for the entire property.

4. **Sublease** is when the Tenant collects the rent from the sublessee and then pays the landlord. A sublease may be for the entire property or just for part of the property.

Duties of the Tenant follow:

1. To pay rent — Usually in money, but sometimes as a share of the crops. It used to be that rent was payable at the end of the term, but usually today the rent is payable at the beginning of the term. If rent is not paid, usually today the landlord cannot seize the tenant's personal property found in the house or on the land.

2. To protect and preserve the property — The tenant must prevent damage or property deterioration.

Rights of the Landlord are:

1. To receive rent.

2. To regain possession — If the tenant will not move, the landlord may go to the judge and get an *Action of Ejectment* permitting the sheriff to eject the tenant. The tenant cannot remove fixtures that have become a part of the real property, such as cupboards that the tenant has nailed to the walls.

3. To enter the property to preserve it — Landlord may enter to fix a leaky roof or to put on a new roof, but landlord cannot show the house to prospective tenants or buyers unless this provision is in the lease.

4. To assign rights — Landlord can assign his benefits *(The Right to Receive Rents)* to another party, but landlord cannot assign responsibilities.

Duties of the Landlord are:

1. To pay taxes and assessments — Unless the lease states otherwise, the Landlord must pay these.

2. To protect the tenant from concealed defects such as: Concealed cisterns, rotting joists, fire escapes.

Lease Termination has legal rules as follows:

1. A lease for a fixed time expires at the end of that time.

2. Tenant can carry fire insurance for the amount of the tenant's possible loss.

3. If the tenant moves out before the lease expires, this is a breach of contract.

4. Forcible Entry and Detainer Action by the landlord can be used as follows: If a tenant refuses to leave the property at the end of the lease, the landlord may enter the property and take *Detainer Action* in court to force the tenant off the property.

Improvements by the Tenant are covered as follows:

1. A tenant may remove an *Improvement,* such as curtains he/she has put up, that are personal property not attached to the land.

2. If a tenant has put up a *Fixture* (something attached to the land, such as a *Henhouse*) the tenant cannot take it with him or her at the end of the lease.

An *Easement* is a right to use a road across another person's land, or perhaps the right to share a driveway with a neighbor. Easements can be obtained by Adverse Use, that is, by using the road for a period of time without the owner's permission if the owner does not object during that time. (If the Owner later objects after the passage of a long period of time, it is too late, and the easement allows the other party to continue using the road.) The period of time is different in the various states.

REVIEW QUESTIONS

1. How does real property differ from personal property?

Real property is land or anything attached to land, like buildings, fences, and perennial plants. Personal property is not permanently attached to the land, like trailers, annual crops, and bicycles.

2. In law, why is it important to determine whether or not a river is navigable?

Landowners own the land under a non-navigable river. On the other hand, if a river is navigable, property owners own only the land down to the low-water mark of the river.

3. How does an Improvement differ from a Fixture?

An improvement is personal property not attached to the land — like curtains in the window. These may be taken with the tenant when moving. Fixtures are improvements which become attached to the land and thus legally become real property — like cupboards. These may not be removed by the tenant when he leaves.

4. Give examples of tangible personal property.

Property which can be touched, like jewelry, motorcycles, autos.

5. Give examples of intangible personal property.

Property which itself cannot be touched — only the evidence of the property ownership can be touched, such as stock certificates, mortgages, bonds.

6. How does a Life Estate in property differ from a Fee Simple Estate?

An owner in fee simple may sell or bequeath the property, while an owner of a life estate cannot.

7. How does a person become the owner of a life estate?

It is given or bequeathed to him by a Grantor.

8. Who is the Remainder in a life estate?

The person who gets the property after the death of the owner of a life estate.

9. What is Consideration?
The duty to do something or pay something in a contract.

10. What does it mean when a person dies intestate?
Without leaving a will.

11. How does the court dispose of a person's property when he or she does die intestate?
According to the individual state's Law of Descent.

12. Let us say that we own land along the bank of a large river which continually washes up silt onto our land, giving us more land. Are we entitled to this new land, and if so, what is the legal term for it?
Yes, we are entitled to the land through accretion.

13. Does the inventor get exclusive use to his invention?
Not unless he or she patents it.

14. How does a patent differ from a copyright?
A Patent protects an invention, such as a new type of mousetrap. It gives the inventor exclusive use to the invention for a number of years. This is done by writing the U.S. Patent Office. A Copyright protects the writer of a new book, magazine article, piece of music, architectural blueprints, etc. by giving the person exclusive use of it for a number of years. This is done by writing the Library of Congress.

15. How does a quitclaim deed differ from a warranty deed?
In a quitclaim deed the former owner says he or she no longer has any ownership in the property, but the person does not guarantee anything else. In a warranty deed the former owner guarantees that there are no title defects.

16. What is a title defect?
A prior claim on the property by one of the former owners

of the property or by someone connected with one of the former owners.

17. What is a Covenant?

A special agreement in the deed. For example, the deed might state that the owner is to share a driveway with the owner of a neighboring piece of property.

18. Why should a deed be recorded at the courthouse?

To prevent the former owner from attempting to sell the property to someone else.

19. Why should a mortgage be recorded at the courthouse?

Recording it would give the mortgagee a prior chance of collecting on the mortgage in case the mortgager mortgaged his property at a later date to someone else.

20. What is a Mortgage?

A lien based on real estate in order to secure a debt.

21. When a property owner makes a mortgage payment, if the agreement does not state otherwise, which gets paid off first — the principal or the interest?

The interest.

22. How does a First Mortgage differ from a Second Mortgage?

The owner of the First Mortgage can collect all that is due him or her from the mortgager before the owner of the Second Mortgage has any rights to collect.

23. What is an Abstract of Title?

A history of the property as far back as possible.

24. Why must the Abstract be brought up to date when the property changes hands?

To assure the new owner that no one else will come out of the past and claim the property.

25. How can a new owner of real property be sure he has exclusive claim to the property?

By buying Title Insurance from an insurance company.

26. What is a Foreclosure Sale?

A sale of the property by the mortgagee, the court, or the sheriff after the mortgager has defaulted on his or her mortgage payments.

27. After the property has been sold in a Foreclosure Sale, do any parties other than the mortgagee have prior claims on this money?

Yes, costs of foreclosure must be paid, as well as taxes, materials furnishers' bills, and mechanics' liens.

28. How does a Mortgage differ from a Trust Deed?

In a mortgage, the mortgagor has title and use of the property. In a trust deed, the title is conveyed to a trustee, who manages the property for the creditors.

29. How does a tenant differ from a lodger?

A tenant has exclusive possession of the property, while a lodger uses the building or part of the building under the supervision of the owner.

30. Does a lease have to be in writing?

Yes, if it is for a period of over a year. However, it should always be in writing to avoid later disputes.

31. How does a Tenancy for Years differ from a Tenancy from Year to Year?

A Tenancy for Years has the date when the tenancy ends mentioned in the contract. A Tenancy from Year to Year does not have a definite ending date.

32. What is an Action of Ejectment?

A court order allowing the sheriff to remove the former tenant.

33. Does a landlord have the right to enter the property that he has rented to the tenant?

Only to preserve the property, like fixing the roof or putting on a new roof.

34. How does a person gain an easement by Adverse Use?

By continuing to use a road across another person's property for the number of years mentioned in the state law.

CHAPTER 15

WILLS AND INHERITANCES

15.1 DEFINITION OF A WILL

A Will is the instructions of a person, recognized by law, which direct the distribution of that person's property at death.

The **Time** at which the instructions in a will go into effect is after the death of the maker of the will. Before a person's death, the person may make any changes in the will that the person wishes.

A **Testator** is a *Man* who makes a will. A **Testatrix** is a *Woman* who makes a will.

An **Executor** (man) or **Executrix** (woman) is a person appointed by the will to administer and distribute the estate.

An **Estate** is all of the property that was owned or controlled by the testator at the time of the testator's death. A *Bequest (Legacy)* is a provision in the will which gives to a named person certain *Personal Property* owned by the testator. A **Devise** is a provision of the will to grant *Real Property* owned by the testator to a person named in the will.

15.2 TYPES OF WILLS

A **Holographic Will** is one written entirely in the handwriting of the testator. It is not recognized in most states unless it complies with other legal requirements of a valid will.

A **Nuncupative Will** is an oral will made to two or more persons in which the testator tells them how he or she wishes the property disposed of. In order to be valid, it must be reduced to writing and signed by the witnesses. Such a will is recognized in about two-thirds of the states, but only for personal property and for a limited amount. It must have been made during the testator's last illness. Such a will may be made by a serviceman or a mariner.

Multiple Wills are several wills executed by the testator. All must be presented at probate. (**Probate** is the official approving of the will as valid in Probate Court.)

15.3 WHO CAN MAKE A WILL?

The privilege of making an enforceable will is granted certain citizens by the state law. In most states a person must be of age (18) and of sound mind. In some states, minors can dispose of personal property by a will, but not real property. Deaf, dumb, illiterate, and blind people can make wills if it can be shown they knew and understood the contents of the will.

15.4 PROVISIONS OF A WILL

The will must express the instructions of the decedent concerning the distribution of the decedent's property and must be signed by the decedent and two or more witnesses. Most wills state that the executor should pay just debts and funeral expenses. Most wills give the name of the executor. Most wills then mention the various legatees and devisees and the amount of property going to them. Many wills mention a RESIDUARY LEGATEE who will receive any money left over after the others have been paid.

15.5 RIGHTS OF WIDOWS

A widow may inherit despite contrary provisions of the will. A widow has a right of dower (part interest in the husband's real property at date of death, all the way from half to all of the property, depending on the state law). In many states the widow can disregard the will and take her intestate share according to the *Law of Descent* in that state — often at least one-third.

15.6 EXECUTION OF A WILL

Rules for the Execution of a Will (the Making of a Will) follow:

1. The Testator tells the witnesses that this is his or her will, but the witnesses do not need to read the will. The witnesses then sign at the end of the will. There are usually two or three witnesses, depending on state law.

2. The Testator signs each page of the will.

15.7 REVOCATION OF A WILL

Can a will be revoked (cancelled)? A testator may revoke a previous will if the testator is of sound mind, by his own free will, with lack of domination, fraud, or duress.

15.8 CODICILS

A **Codicil** is a formal document which amends or changes the provisions of a former or present will.

15.9 INTESTACY

Intestacy is dying without a will. Distribution of real property of an intestate is determined by the law of the state in which the real property is located. Distribution of personal property of an intestate is determined by the place where the intestate made his home.

Usually the surviving spouse gets from one-third to one-half of the estate, depending on the state law. The children get the rest. If there are no children, then the surviving spouse gets the whole estate. If there is no surviving spouse, the estate will be divided between children and grandchildren.

If there is a surviving spouse, usually (depending on state law) the children and grandchildren will get from half to two-thirds of the estate.

Per Capita Basis is as follows: Each surviving child or grandchild will get the same proportionate share.

Per Stirpes Basis is as follows: Any children of a deceased child (actually grandchildren of the testator) generally would take the share that the deceased child would have been entitled to inherit.

If the deceased leaves neither spouse nor descendants, the estate then will be divided among parents (ascendants), if living. If not, then between surviving brothers and sisters. If not, then to nephews and nieces. Adopted children are counted, but not stepchildren.

If there are no relatives at all, the estate goes to the State.

15.10 PROBATE OF AN ESTATE

Probate of an Estate starts with a hearing in Probate Court. (Probate is the official proving of a will as authentic. Probate Court is a special court with the power over the administration of wills.)

First there is a determination as to whether or not there is a will and the will's containing the name of the administrator of the estate.

If there is no will, a relative of the deceased will petition the court to be appointed administrator.

In a Contested Will, if anyone questions the execution of the will, or the testamentary intent, or the capacity of the decedent, the judge must come to a decision.

Administration of the Estate by the personal representative then takes place.

— Notice of the estate probate is printed in the newspaper so that all creditors may present their claims within six months.

— A temporary award of money is made to the surviving spouse so that the spouse can have money while the will is being probated.

— The Administrator inventories all the assets and establishes their value.

If there are enough assets, the administrator pays funeral and burial expenses, the expenses of the decedent's last illness, the administration costs of the estate, the debts of the decedent and the taxes owed.

Estate Tax is due the federal government based on the value of the estate. Today the Federal Estate Tax has large exemptions so for all except the largest estates there is no federal estate tax. The amount of this exemption changes from time to time. Transfers of property from one spouse to another are usually exempt from this tax.

State Inheritance Taxes are assessed on property that each beneficiary receives from the decedent. The closer the relationship between the beneficiary and the decedent, the lower the inheritance tax will be.

The administrator supplies the court with an accounting. After the court approves, the administrator distributes the remaining property and money to the beneficiaries.

15.11 ESTATE PLANNING

Trusts are written documents giving legal title to property to a trustee who must administer the property according to the terms of the documents and for the benefit of the beneficiaries named in the trust.

An **Inter Vivos Trust** is established by a living person.

A **Testamentary Trust** is established in a will.

A **Revocable Trust** is a trust wherein the establisher can change or completely do away with the trust, or change the administrator.

An **Irrevocable Trust** cannot be changed. The trustee, not the person creating the trust, must pay the taxes on income earned by the trust property. Advantages:

1. When the creator dies, there are no estate taxes, no probate fees, since the trust is not a part of the estate.

2. Professional property management by a trustee, often the Trust Department of a bank, manages the trust.

   Disadvantages: There are management fees for the trust.

Joint Property and Estate Planning is established based on

the form of tenancy involved. In the case of Joint Tenants with Rights of Survivorship, if two persons have a bank account as joint tenants, and one dies, the other gets the full amount in the account, and it is not probated.

When there are Tenants in Common, if two persons have a bank account as tenants in common and one dies, half the account goes into the estate of the deceased, and the other half of the account goes to the surviving person.

Tenants in the Entirety means ownership of property jointly between husband and wife only and is a special term for Joint Tenants with Rights of Survivorship.

Life insurance benefits are not subject to income taxes or estate or inheritance taxes.

Custodial Accounts and Estate Planning Accounts are usually set up for minor children as a way to escape income, estate, and inheritance taxes.

REVIEW QUESTIONS

1. **When does a will have legal effect?**
After the death of the maker.

2. **When can a person change his will?**
At any time he wishes.

3. **Who is the Executor of a will?**
The person appointed in the will to administer and distribute the estate.

4. **Who is a Testatrix?**
A woman making a will.

5. **What is an estate?**
The property owned by a person at the time of death.

6. What is the difference between a Bequest and a Devise?

A bequest is a provision in the will leaving certain *personal* property to beneficiaries, while a devise is a provision in the will leaving certain *real* property to beneficiaries.

7. What is a Holographic Will?

One in the maker's handwriting.

8. Are Holographic Wills usually legally valid?

No, unless they comply with all the other legal requirements of wills.

9. What is a Nuncupative Will?

An oral will made in the presence of two or more witnesses.

10. What types of people can make wills in the U.S.?

People at least 18 years of age and of sound mind.

11. Who is a legatee?

A person receiving personal property in a will.

12. Who is a residuary legatee?

The person receiving any extra money in a will, after all the other beneficiaries have received their portions as mentioned in the will.

13. What is dower?

The rights of a widow in the estate of her deceased husband. This has to do with his real property, and, depending on the state, it runs from half to all the real property at date of husband's death.

14. What is the Law of Descent?

Laws passed by the various states determining how the property should be distributed for a person dying without a will.

15. What is a Codicil?

A formal document amending the will's provisions.

16. What is Intestacy?

Dying without leaving a will.

17. If a husband dies without a will, how much will his widow get of his property?

This depends on state law. If there are no children, she may get the entire estate. If there are children, she may get from one-third to one-half of the estate.

18. Why are notices of estates being probated printed in the newspaper?

So all creditors will know about it and be able to present their claims for payment.

19. Do witnesses to the will need to read the will?

No.

20. In distributing the deceased's property to children and grandchildren how does the Per Capita Basis differ from the Per Stirpes Basis?

In the Per Capita Basis, each child or grandchild gets his or her proportionate share. In the Per Stirpes Basis, any children of a deceased child generally would take the share that the deceased child would have been entitled to inherit.

21. If the deceased leaves no will and has no spouse or children, who is usually next in line to inherit?

The parents of the deceased.

22. If the deceased leaves no will, has no spouse or children or parents living, who will inherit?

Surviving brothers and sisters, and if none of these, nephews and nieces related by blood.

23. If a person dies without a will, will stepchildren become beneficiaries?

No, but adopted children will.

24. What is the purpose of the first hearing in Probate Court?

To determine whether or not the deceased has a will, and to

appoint an administrator of the estate, if there is no will.

25. What is one of the administrator's first jobs?

To determine the assets of the estate.

26. What is the purpose of the final hearing in Probate Court?

To give the court an accounting of the assets of the estate, and to get permission from the court to distribute the assets according to the terms of the will.

27. Why is Estate Planning important?

Inheritance and tax laws change, and estate planning is consulting with a lawyer for the best methods for people to cut down on their taxes legally. People also do this by consulting with tax advisors.

28. What are trusts?

Written documents giving legal title to property to a trustee to administer according to the directions in the trust.

29. Why are trusts sometimes beneficial in cutting down taxes?

When the maker of the trust dies, the assets in the trust are not part of the estate, so they do not go through probate.

30. How do Joint Tenants differ from Tenants in Common?

Joint Tenancy carries with it the right of survivorship, while Tenants in Common split assets equally between the estate and the surviving party in case of the death of one of the parties.

31. How do insurance contracts and custodial accounts help in estate planning?

They are methods of legally cutting down income and death taxes.

CHAPTER 16

PARTNERSHIPS

16.1   DEFINITION OF A PARTNERSHIP

A **partnership** is an agreement between two or more persons to carry on a business for profit.

Partnership agreements may be oral or written. However, they must be written if they are to last over a year, or if they involve the buying or selling of real estate.

Partnerships are not separate legal entities in most states.

Each partner is subject to unlimited liability for partnership debts. (This means a partner must sometimes pay more than what he or she has invested.)

A partner cannot transfer his or her interest without the consent of all the other partners.

Unless otherwise stated in the partnership agreement, each partner has a direct and equal voice in the management of the business.

Partnership is ended by agreement, death, bankruptcy, or withdrawal.

Each partner pays an income tax on his or her share of the

net profits whether distributed or not. This is reported both on the partnership tax form and on the personal tax returns of each partner. The partnership as such pays no income tax, but each partner must pay income tax on his or her share of the partnership income as reported on the personal return.

16.2   JOINT VENTURE

A **Joint Venture** is similar to a partnership, except it is for a single transaction or for a series of transactions.

EXAMPLE

James Smith and Bill Brown set up a joint venture to run a candy booth at the county fair, which lasts a week.

16.3   LIMITED PARTNERSHIP

A **Limited Partnership** must have at least one general partner who has unlimited liability. Limited partners do not usually manage the business and do not have unlimited liability. The articles of partnership must be filed with an officer of government according to state law, usually in the office of the Secretary of State in the state capital.

16.4   COOPERATIVES

Cooperatives are unions of individuals for the carrying on of some productive enterprise, and profits are shared in accordance with the capital or labor contributed by each. Some states have laws regulating cooperatives.

EXAMPLE

Farmers' Cooperatives.

16.5   UNIFORM PARTNERSHIP ACT

The Uniform Partnership Act has been adopted by most states and sets up rules regulating partnerships.

16.6   PARTNERSHIP PROPERTY

Partnership Property is all property originally brought into the partnership, and all property brought in later by purchase or gift is partnership property, such as land, cash, merchandise, corporate stock.

Goodwill is public favor and patronage built up by the owner or former owner of a business.

Both personal and real property may be owned by a partnership.

All partners have rights in the partnership property (trucks, factory equipment, buildings). Partners, in the absence of an agreement to the contrary, have equal rights to use the partnership assets in partnership business. But the partners cannot use this property for any other purpose without the consent of the other partners.

Partners may *assign* their benefits in the partnership, such as profits, to someone else, but this person does not thereby become a partner and has no right to manage the partnership.

The creditors of a partner may get a court order appointing a receiver to take over the liable partner's benefits in a partnership.

If a partner dies, the other partners have the right to carry on liquidation proceedings, so the deceased partner's heirs get their share eventually.

16.7 POWERS, RIGHTS, DUTIES, AND LIABILITIES OF PARTNERS

Partners share profits equally, or in the way set out in the Articles of Partnership. Losses are shared the same way as profits.

Partners who have made advances to the partnership beyond those of other partners are to be repaid those advances before anything is distributed to other partners.

If a partner, in doing partnership business, spent money of his or her own for the partnership, this partner must be reimbursed by the partnership.

Unless stated otherwise, all partners have equal rights in the management of the partnership and in access to partnership books.

The partners have a fiduciary relationship to one another and must account to one another for their actions.

The partnership is liable for partners' torts while they are transacting partnership business.

EXAMPLE

A partner on partnership business drives a partnership car and hits another car. The driver of the other car could sue the partnership.

Partnerships cannot usually be sued for criminal liability since they are not legal persons. However, there are exceptions.

EXAMPLE

If a hospital is a partnership, it might be criminally liable for allowing an unauthorized person to perform an operation within the hospital.

General partners have unlimited liability to the full extent of their personal assets.

16.8   PARTNERSHIP DISSOLUTION

After a partnership is dissolved, no new business should be undertaken; however, old business can be completed and the business can be wound down.

Other partners can be taken in and a new partnership formed.

If the partnership is to be *Liquidated,* assets are sold for cash, debts are paid, and if there is enough money, partners are paid.

Methods of Dissolving a Partnership are: by agreement between the partners, by any one partner wanting to leave, by illegality.

EXAMPLE
A liquor store would have to go out of business if prohibition began.

A partnership also dissolves if any of the partners or the partnership itself becomes *Bankrupt,* if partners are citizens of nations at war with each other, in cases of misappropriation of funds by a partner, insanity of a partner, or serious dissention among partners.

Order of payment upon **Liquidation** follows:

1.   All assets are sold for cash.

2.   All creditors are then paid, other than partners.

3. Loans of partners are then paid to partners.

4. Partners are paid according to their capital accounts.

REVIEW QUESTIONS

1. Even though oral partnership agreements are often legal, why is it better to have them in writing?

This prevents future disagreements as to the original intent of the parties.

2. What is Unlimited Liability?

If the partnership cannot pay its debts, the partners must dig into their own personal funds to pay partnership creditors.

3. Do partnerships as such pay a federal income tax?

No, but each partner must report his or her proportionate share of the partnership income on his or her income tax, and the partnership itself must file a partnership tax form.

4. If the partnership agreement states nothing about which partner shall manage the business, how is this determined?

Each partner then has equal say as to the management.

5. How does a Joint Venture differ from a partnership?

A joint venture is usually for a shorter length of time.

6. How do limited partnerships differ from general partnerships?

In a general partnership, all partners have unlimited liability. In a limited partnership, one or more partners have unlimited liability, and the rest of the partners have only limited liability. Also, most states require limited partnerships to file articles of partnership agreements.

7. What is meant by Limited Liability?

Partners with Limited Liability can lose only as much as they have invested in the business and no more.

8. How are profits shared in a partnership?

According to the instructions in the Articles of Partnership. If there are no instructions regarding profit-sharing, then each partner gets an equal share of the profits.

9. How are profits shared in a farmers' cooperative?

According to the Articles or Bylaws of the cooperative. Usually this depends on the amount of business that an individual does with the cooperative during the year.

10. Why is Goodwill an asset of a business?

If a business buys an asset for more than it is worth, the difference is the asset, Goodwill. This is supposed to be the public favor built up by the previous owner of the business.

11. Who owns the assets of the partnership?

They are owned by the partnership itself and can be used for partnership business. Partners cannot use these assets for their personal whims without the approval of all the other partners.

12. Can a personal creditor of a partner get control of the partner's investment in the partnership itself?

Yes, with a court order appointing a receiver for the partner's share of the partnership property.

13. If a partner dies, does this dissolve the partnership?

Yes, but the other partners have the right to close out the partnership or to take in a new partner and continue with the business, as long as the heirs of the deceased partner derive the value of the deceased partner's share of the business.

14. Why is a partnership a fiduciary relationship?

Each partner trusts the other partners to be honest and faithful in the work of the partnership, in handling money and other property, and in relations with their partners.

15. How does Partnership Dissolution differ from Partnership Liquidation?

When a partner dies or wants to leave, this is Dissolution.

Then other partners wind up the business. After the assets are sold for cash, and the cash is used to pay the partnership debts and to pay the capital accounts of the partners, this is liquidation.

16. If one partner dies, and the other partners select another person to become partner in his place, is this Dissolution or Liquidation?

Dissolution.

CHAPTER 17

CORPORATIONS

17.1 THE NATURE OF CORPORATIONS

Corporations are legal entities with a separate legal existence from shareholders.

They may sue and be sued.

A corporation has Limited Liability. This means that shareholders and officers of a corporation cannot lose more than they have invested in the corporation.

EXCEPTION

Officers or stockholders who use a corporation to carry out fraud, crime, or defeat a public convenience are personally liable.

17.2 TYPES OF CORPORATIONS

De Jure (according to law) — A De Jure Corporation is one that is formed in compliance with all the important provisions of the state incorporation law.

De Facto (in fact) — A De Facto Corporation is one that has been formed without compliance with all the important provisions of the state incorporation law.

— There has to have been a "good faith" attempt to establish the corporation in conformance with the state incorporation law.

— The business must have made transactions as a corporation.

A **De Facto Corporation** can act as a corporation until it is dissolved by state action.

Corporation by Estoppel — An organization that holds itself out to be a corporation cannot later back out from a business transaction by denying that it is a corporation.

Private Corporations are those organized for private purposes and in order to make a profit, such as General Motors.

Public Corporations are those for public purposes, such as counties, cities, school districts.

Nonprofit Corporations are for religious, educational, charitable, social or cemetery purposes, like a church. They do not have stockholders.

A **Domestic Corporation** is one chartered within the state.

A **Foreign Corporation** is one chartered outside the state but doing business within the state.

A **Close Corporation** is one where the entire outstanding stock is held by only one or a few people and is not generally available to the public.

A **Professional Corporation** is one organized by professional people such as doctors or dentists. These skilled professionals cannot avoid personal liability. Usually they are incorporated for tax purposes.

17.3 FORMATION OF A CORPORATION

The people wanting to form a corporation meet with a lawyer who looks up the state incorporation law and fills out a charter form giving the following information: name of corporation, period of existence (can be perpetual), purpose, number of authorized shares, par value, preferred and common stock, address of corporate office, names of at least three of the original incorporators.

This information plus a fee is sent to the Secretary of State at the state capital.

If all is in order, the Secretary of State issues the charter and the corporation can begin legally transacting business.

The Directors have a meeting, where they elect officers, set up bylaws, and begin issuing stock.

Bylaws are set up by a corporation to govern its own internal affairs and are not usually filed with the state or county.

17.4 TERMINATION OF A CORPORATION

A corporation can be ended either voluntarily or involuntarily.

Voluntary ending of a corporation must be approved by a majority of stockholders.

In a corporate *Merger,* one or more corporations are taken over by the surviving corporation. Debts and obligations of the other corporations are taken over by the surviving corporation. Majority of shareholders of the corporations and the boards of directors must approve the merger.

In a corporate *Consolidation,* a new corporation with a new name is formed. Assets and liabilities of the old corporations are taken over by the new corporation. Majority approval of stockholders and boards of directors must be obtained. Shareholders of the old corporations receive stock in the new corporation.

Voluntary Dissolution is brought about by a vote of a majority to two-thirds of the shareholders, depending on state law.

— A certificate of election to dissolve the corporation is filed with the Secretary of State in the state capital.

— The corporation stops carrying on new business transactions.

— The directors sell the assets of the corporation for cash.

— The directors pay off the liabilities of the corporation.

— The directors distribute the remaining cash to the shareholders.

— The directors then file a certificate with the Secretary of State showing that the corporation is terminated.

Involuntary Dissolution of a corporation:

— This can be caused by creditors of a corporation forcing it into bankruptcy.

— It can also be caused by a minority of stockholders (10-50%) petitioning the state for dissolution for such reasons as: Fraud of the Directors, Wasting Corporate Property, Misapplication of Corporate Property, Mismanagement,

Abuse of Authority, and Unfairness to Minority Stockholders.

— The State can dissolve a corporation chartered in the state for such things as: Abuse of Powers and Failure to Pay Franchise Tax.

17.5 CORPORATE MANAGEMENT

The **Express Powers** of a corporation are: To have a corporate name, perpetual existence, to hold property for corporate purposes, to make bylaws governing the corporation, to borrow money for corporate purposes, to sell or mortgage or lease corporate property, to make contracts, to incur liabilities, to conduct its business, to acquire its own shares, to declare and pay dividends, to amend its articles of incorporation, to bring about a merger or consolidation.

The **Implied Powers** of a corporation are: to take and hold property, to borrow money, to loan money of the corporation, to reacquire its own shares of stock, to acquire and hold shares of stock of other corporations, to contribute to charity.

Ultra Vires **Acts** are those beyond the powers of a corporation (such as a private corporation set up originally to make a profit going out and starting a church or school). Today a corporation may contract and go beyond its legal powers, but then must suffer the consequences in a lawsuit.

Shareholders (Stockholders) are people who own one or more shares of stock in a corporation.

— They are entitled to vote on extraordinary corporate transactions *such as a Merger, or Selling of Corporate Assets.*

— They are entitled to *Vote for Members of the Board of Directors.*

— They are entitled to *Receive Dividends* declared by the Board of Directors.

In most corporations, a stockholder gets one vote for each share of stock owned.

— Shareholders who cannot attend stockholders' meetings can vote by proxy. The proxy must be in writing and signed by the shareholder.

— Shareholders may initiate resolutions to be voted on at shareholder meetings.

— Shareholders may inspect the books of the corporation for any legal purpose.

— Shareholders may sue the corporation.

— Shareholders have the right to buy and sell shares in the corporation.

— Shareholders have the right to receive any balance of the net corporate assets upon dissolution of the corporation.

— Shareholders are not personally liable for the debts of the corporation.

Directors (at least 3), are chosen by the stockholders. They may be removed by stockholders for causes of *Insanity, Conviction of a Felony, Fraud, Abuse of Authority.*

Directors cannot vote themselves salaries, but often their salaries are set by articles of incorporation or by shareholder resolutions.

The usual powers of directors are to select corporate policies and to generally manage the affairs of the business:

— Select, supervise, remove, and fix compensation of officers.

— Determine dividend payments.

— Decide on products, prices, services, wages, and labor relations.

Directors must act as a board, not individually.

Directors must usually attend the board meetings and cannot vote by proxy. The corporation needs the value of their consultation and collective judgment.

Directors are *Fiduciaries* and must act in good faith for the corporation's benefit. They are liable to the corporation for *Negligence* or for engaging in *ultra vires* activities ***beyond the powers of the Corporation.***

EXAMPLE

Examples of wrongful acts of directors: False Reports, Improper Expenditure of Corporate Funds, Making Unauthorized Loans.

Officers of a Corporation are chosen by the Board of Directors. (Sometimes they are elected by shareholders.) They can be removed with or without cause by the directors. Usually director-officers receive compensation on a prearranged basis. (Often they get fixed salaries, liberal expense accounts, profit-sharing plans, stock bonuses, pensions, and deferred compensation plans.)

— Officers are usually president, vice president, secretary, and treasurer.

— President is second in command to the chairman of the Board of Directors. Often these two positions are combined. The president has authority to act as agent of the corporation.

— Vice Presidents are usually department heads in large corporations.

— The Secretary keeps records of corporation meetings and transactions.

— The Treasurer handles the money and the controller keeps the records.

— Officers are fiduciaries of the corporation and cannot make secret profits for themselves.

17.6 CORPORATE FINANCE

Corporate Finance is the method corporations use to get money to operate.

Bonds are long-term promissory notes issued to people who lend money to the corporation. Some bonds can be converted into shares of stock of the same corporation. Most bonds are sold by government agencies or by large corporations.

Stocks are shares of ownership of a corporation. Stockholders have indirect control of the corporation, receive dividends, and vote for corporate directors.

The **Stock Certificate** lists the state of incorporation, the name of the stockholder, the number of shares, the class of shares (common or preferred), and the amount of the par value, if any.

Authorized Shares are the number of shares that the state in which the corporation is chartered allows the corporation to issue.

Outstanding Shares are the number of shares that the corporation has issued to the shareholders which are still in the hands of shareholders.

Treasury Shares are the stock originally issued to shareholders but now repurchased by the corporation. They cannot be voted and do not receive dividends.

Common Stock is the ordinary stock of the corporation. Common stockholders are entitled to declared dividends, and upon dissolution, to their share of any remaining assets of the corporation. The common stockholders usually have voting rights, so they choose the Board of Directors. Common stockholders have the greatest gamble, because they lose most if the corporation does poorly and they gain most if the corporation does well.

Preferred Stock usually has preference as to dividends. That is, they get paid dividends before the common stockholders get their dividends, if any. Sometimes preferred stockholders are also preferred as to distribution of capital upon corporate dissolution. Preferred stock is usually cumulative; that is, if the preferred dividends are not paid when due, all the back preferred dividends must be paid before the common stockholders get their dividends. Preferred stockholders can usually vote on *Extraordinary Corporate Decisions,* such as *Sale of Corporate Assets,* or *Corporate Dissolution.*

REVIEW QUESTIONS

1. Which type of business is more closely controlled by the government—partnerships or corporations?

Corporations.

2. How does the nature of a corporation differ from the nature of a partnership?

Corporations are separate legal entities from their stockholders, whereas partnerships are not separate legal entities from the various partners.

3. What is meant by the term *Limited Liability*?

A stockholder of a corporation cannot lose more than that person has invested in the corporation when a corporation runs into financial difficulty.

4. How does a *De Jure* Corporation differ from a *De Facto* Corporation?

A *De Jure* Corporation has been formed in accordance with all the important provisions of the state law, whereas a *De Facto* Corporation has been formed without complying with all the important provisions of the law.

5. Would a state university be an example of a public corporation?

Yes.

6. Would a parish church be an example of a nonprofit corporation?

Yes, many parish churches have incorporation charters from the state.

7. As far as Iowa residents are concerned, what type of corporation is one chartered in Nebraska?

A foreign corporation.

8. Do medical doctors incorporate in order to cut down on malpractice liabilities?

No, a professional corporation cannot help them in this

way. They usually incorporate in order to cut down on taxes legally.

9. In most states, what is the fewest number of people that can legally start a corporation?

Three.

10. Who elects the Board of Directors of a corporation?

The stockholders.

11. How does a Corporate Merger differ from a Corporate Consolidation?

In a merger, one or more corporations are taken over by the surviving corporation, and the surviving corporation keeps its name. In a consolidation, two or more corporations unite, but a new corporation with a new name is formed.

12. How can a corporation be ended involuntarily?

Bankruptcy, abuse of powers, failure to pay franchise tax, fraud, abuse of authority, etc.

13. What are Ultra Vires Acts of a corporation?

Those beyond the authority of the corporation, such as carrying on another type of business, or starting a church.

14. Do stockholders run the corporation?

Only indirectly.

15. What are the rights of stockholders?

To receive dividends and to vote for directors, as well as to vote on extraordinary corporate transactions like whether or not to merge with another corporation.

16. Are shareholders allowed to inspect the books of a corporation?

Yes.

17. Is the day-to-day business of a corporation managed by the Board of Directors?

Not usually. They mainly set overall policy.

18. Can directors vote by proxy?
Not usually.

19. Who runs the day-to-day business of the corporation?
Officers.

20. How are corporate officers chosen?
By the Board of Directors.

21. When a corporation is first organized, how is it usually financed?
By the sale of stocks and bonds.

22. How do stocks differ from bonds?
Stocks are shares of ownership in a corporation, while bonds are evidences that people have loaned money to a corporation.

23. How do Authorized Shares differ from Outstanding Shares?
Authorized shares are the number of shares that the corporate charter, approved by the state, allows the corporation to issue. Outstanding shares are the number of shares of the corporate stock actually in the hands of shareholders.

24. What are Treasury Shares?
Former outstanding stock of the corporation which the corporation has bought back from the stockholders.

25. Do Treasury Shares receive dividends?
No.

26. How does Preferred Stock differ from common stock?
Preferred Stock usually gets first chance at dividends, and at corporate assets in case of dissolution. Common stockholders usually get to vote for corporate officers.

CHAPTER 18

THE LEGAL ENVIRONMENT OF BUSINESS

18.1 PRODUCT LIABILITY

Product Liability is getting more important in modern society. Because of the possibility of large judgments, a company can no longer safely decide that a cheap, unsafe product will bring the greatest profits.

A manufacturer who fails to exercise reasonable care in the manufacture of goods is subject to liability for physical harm to the user of the product.

EXAMPLE

Children's toys, blankets, automobiles.

A manufacturer must exercise due care in the design of all products.

EXAMPLE

An electric fan must have a screen to protect users from the rotating metal blade.

Manufacturers must **Test and Inspect** their products for safety before selling them.

Many times a manufacturer should **Place a Warning Statement** on the manufactured products. They must also include **Dangers of Misuse**.

EXAMPLE

Warning regarding gasoline taken internally. Warning about keeping fingers away from power mower.

18.2   ELECTRONIC TRANSFERS OF FUNDS

Electronic Transfer of Funds is carried on rapidly by machines.

Consumers have cards that give them access to a bank machine, and they have secret numbers that they punch into the machine.

In some stores there are point-of-sale terminals. The customer gives a personal debit card to the store clerk who uses it in the store machine, and this transfers money from the customer's bank account to the store account.

Automated Tellers outside banks allow customers to deposit, transfer, or withdraw money at any time of the day or night.

On-Line Cash Dispensers are connected to a central-processing computer that has access to the consumer's account. It is complex but gives the consumer immediate cash from the account.

Pay-by-Phone System is used by consumers to pay utility bills. The consumer phones the bank and orders the bank to pay the persons or businesses that the consumer specifies.

Preauthorized Direct Deposits are made by an agreement

between the recipient and employer (or in case of social security checks, between the recipient and the federal government) so that the payer deposits money in the account of the recipient at stated times.

The Electronic Fund Transfer Act of 1978:

— States that at the time the customer contracts for these services, the financial institution must disclose customer liabilities such as financial charges imposed, right to stop payment, and the liability of the institution to the consumer.

— Requires documentation. Whenever there is an electronic transfer, the financial institution must provide the customer with such information as: date of transfer, amount of money involved, customer's account, identity of any third party to whom money was transferred, location of the terminal involved.

— Requires that preauthorized transfers recurring at regular intervals (like house payments) must have customer's written agreement. Customer can stop payment if customer gives financial institution oral or written notice within three days of the date of payment.

— Requires that financial institution must give customers periodic statements.

— Error Resolution. Within 60 days of receiving a periodic statement containing an error, a customer must notify the financial institution in writing, and the financial institution has 10 days to investigate the error and report back to the customer.

— The customer must notify the financial institution within two days after the loss or theft of the customer's card, then the customer is liable for only the lesser of $50 or the amount of the transfer.

— The financial institution is liable to the customer for all damages proximately caused by its failure to make an electronic fund transfer.

EXCEPTIONS

If the electronic terminal does not have sufficient cash or the customer does not have sufficient funds in customer account, or "good faith" error.

18.3 SECURITY INTEREST

A **Security Interest** is where the seller and buyer sign an agreement giving the seller an interest in the purchased property until the buyer has fully paid for it. Another example of *Security Interest* is collateral for a bank loan.

In order for the seller to *Establish a Security Interest,* three things must happen:

1. The buyer and seller agree that the secured party (seller) has a security interest.

2. The debtor receives value (usually the merchandise).

3. The debtor has rights in the collateral (usually possession).

Unless the goods are in the hands of the seller, the Security Agreement must be *In Writing.* The agreement should reasonably define the collateral.

The Security Agreement should also include *The Amount of Debt, Terms of Payment, Responsibility for Care of Collateral, Acceleration of Payment Rights,* and *Right to Additional Collateral.*

Perfecting security interest in the collateral is putting the world on notice that the seller or creditor has special interest in the collateral.

— This is done by *Filing a Financing Statement at the Courthouse.*

— This could also be done by the seller taking possession of the collateral.

EXAMPLE

Lender borrows $10,000 from the bank and puts up some of lender's stock certificates for collateral, and the banker then files these in the bank vault.

If the buyer defaults, and two or more creditors claim the same property, the creditor who filed the financing statement first has the prior claim.

Collateral is security pledged as payment of a loan.

18.4   BANKRUPTCY

Bankruptcy Laws are federal laws providing relief and protection to the debtor while fairly distributing the debtor's assets among creditors.

The Bankruptcy Reform Act of 1978 set a federal bankruptcy court up in each federal court district.

The Bankruptcy Judge appoints a temporary trustee, or later the creditors appoint a permanent trustee, to handle the assets of the bankrupt party.

In **Voluntary Bankruptcy**, legal proceedings are started by the *Debtor.*

In **Involuntary Bankruptcy**, legal proceedings are started by the *Creditor.* For Involuntary Bankruptcy, there must be claims of at least $5,000 against a debtor.

The **Trustee** takes all the bankrupt's assets as of the date of filing the bankruptcy petition, sells them for cash, and distributes the cash to the creditors according to the priorities established by the bankruptcy law, Chapter 7.

— Property acquired by the bankrupt within 180 days *after* filing the petition is also distributed.

— If the bankrupt has transferred property to one creditor in preference to other creditors when the debtor (the bankrupt) was insolvent, the trustee can void these transfers and bring this property into the bankruptcy proceedings.

Some property is exempt from bankruptcy proceedings and may be kept by the bankrupt debtor. These are: Debtor's residence, up to a value of $7,500; Debtor's motor vehicle, up to a value of $1,200; household furnishings, wearing apparel, appliances, books, musical instruments, animals, personal crops up to $200 in value, $500 in jewelry, $400 interest in any property, $750 in implements, tools of trade, or professional books, unmatured life insurance policies, $4,000 accrued interest or dividends on life insurance policies, prescribed health aids, right to unemployment compensation, Social Security, Veterans' Benefits, Disability Benefits; Debtor's interest in any other property up to $400.

Each class of claims is paid in full before any payment is made of claims of lower priority. If there is not enough money to pay fully all claims in any class, the money available is prorated among the creditors in that class.

Secured Creditors can claim their property first.

Fees of administering the bankruptcy proceedings are paid next. (These include: Legal Fees, Accounting Fees, Trustee Fees, Court Costs.)

Then expenses of the debtor's business and financial affairs are paid.

Next, claims for wages, salaries, or commissions earned by employees within 90 days before the filing of the petitions or the cessation of the debtor's business are paid, with claims given priority up to $2,000 per individual.

Then claims for contributions to an employee benefit plan are paid, with limits up to $2,000 per individual.

Then deposits made on consumer goods or services that were not received are repaid.

Next, tax claims submitted by governmental units are paid.

Next, if a claim exceeds the amount allowed as a priority, it becomes a *General Claim.*

General Claims are examined next. After all classes of priority have been paid, any remaining property is distributed on a pro rata basis to all unsecured creditors with general claims against the debtor's estate.

Discharge of Debts is the next step. The Court may then discharge the individual debtor from all his or her debts, although the debtor will not be discharged if debtor has gone through bankruptcy proceedings within six years of filing the petition, or if the debtor has intentionally concealed assets.

Partnerships and corporations are not discharged from debts under the 1978 federal bankruptcy law. They can seek to reorganize, or they may seek to liquidate under state laws.

Discharge relieves the debtor from any obligation for the payment of debts that arose prior to the filing of the petition except: Claims for back taxes that arose within three years prior to the bankruptcy, claims from embezzlement, fraud, or larceny of the debtor, tort claims, alimony or child support claims, fines and penalties, and educational loans becoming due less than five years prior to the filing of the bankruptcy petition.

Business Reorganization under Chapter 11 of the Bankruptcy Act is a possibility.

— The business can still continue to operate.

— The Court appoints a Creditors' Committee usually made up of the seven largest creditors.

— The debtor may file a plan for reorganization.

— The creditors may request the court that a trustee be appointed.

— After the Court has determined that all creditors are to be treated as fairly as possible under the proposed plan, the Court may approve it. This then binds debtors and creditors.

Relieving the Family Farmer is provided for under one section of the Federal Bankruptcy Act. In order to be eligible for this relief from the demands of creditors, the Family Farmer must have a regular annual income, and over 50% of the annual gross income must be from farming operations.

— The debtor can reorganize, remain in possession of his or her property, and file a plan for reorganization.

— The farmer's future income is to be subject to control by the *Trustee.*

— All priority claims are to be paid in full, within three (sometimes five) years.

Regular Income Plans In Bankruptcy. Chapter 13 of the Bankruptcy Law allows this. (Chapter 13 is used by individuals with regular incomes who owe debts and want to pay them without harassment by creditors. This chapter can be used by wage earners and/or by people with incomes from investments, social security, and pensions, with unsecured debts of less than $100,000, and secured debts of less than $350,000.)

— There is a **Voluntary Petition** of the debtor that starts these proceedings.

— An **Automatic Stay** stops creditors from taking action against the debtor.

— The debtor proposes a plan providing for the use of the future income for the payment of creditors.

— The income will be subject to control by a Trustee.

— The plan must insure that all claims entitled to priority are paid in full.

— Unsecured creditors are divided into classes, but all claims within any class must be treated the same.

— Claimants may be paid in full or paid an amount not less than what they would receive in a liquidation proceeding.

— Creditors are to be paid within three (sometimes five) years.

— A "good faith" requirement must be met before the court will agree to the plan.

18.5 SECURITIES REGULATION

Securities Regulation has become much more strict in recent years.

Securities are Contracts where a person invests money in a common enterprise, with expectation of profit, solely from the efforts of the promoter but not from the investors themselves.

Securities cannot be sold until they have been registered with the Securities and Exchange Commission. A prospectus, giving detailed information regarding the securities, must be filed with the SEC and also given to interested investors.

Ten days before a corporation mails proxies to its stockholders, the corporation must file a copy of the proxy with the Securities and Exchange Commission. Then the SEC often issues informal letters to the corporation requiring some changes before the proxies are mailed.

The SEC requires that the corporation furnish the stockholders all important information concerning the matter being submitted to them for their vote.

If any shareholders want to present matters before the corporation's annual meeting, and if they give the corporation timely notice, the SEC requires management to include these proposals in its proxy statements.

A **Proxy** is a written statement whereby a holder of securities gives permission to another person to vote the stockholder's shares at the annual meeting.

Williams Act of the 1960's was set up to regulate hostile corporate takeovers and insider trading. It mentioned that any person or group that acquires more than 5% of a class of securities registered under the Exchange Act is required to file a statement with the SEC and the issuing company within 10 days and must include: The person or group background and the number of share owners, its purpose in acquiring the stock, the source of funds used to buy the security, its plans for the targeted company, and any contracts or understandings with individuals or groups relevant to the targeted company.

If there is a hostile tender offer or takeover bid, the targeted company must also file a statement of its attempt to defeat the takeover.

To prevent short-swing profits by insiders, the law also requires that directors, officers, and owners of 10% of the securities of an issuing corporation cannot realize profits on stocks by buying and selling within a six-month period. Any such realized profits must be returned to the corporation.

18.6 ANTITRUST LAWS

Antitrust Laws were set up to halt monopolies and price fixing. Trusts are monopolies or near-monopolies in a field that become so powerful that they control prices and production.

The **Sherman Act of 1890** condemns conspiracies in restraint of trade, vertical and horizontal price fixing, group boycotts, and division of markets, in interstate and foreign commerce.

The **Clayton Act of 1914** prohibits price discrimination. It prohibits mergers that tend to bring on monopolies.

The **Robinson-Patman Act of 1936** prohibits price discrimination.

These laws are enforced by the Department of Justice through injunctions (court orders) and fines.

Unions are exempt from antitrust laws. Farmers' cooperatives and the sport of baseball are also exempt.

Regulated industries (such as public utilities) are exempt from antitrust laws.

Boycotts are refusals to buy from a certain company. They are illegal if done in collusion by a concerted group.

Tying Agreements (also called Tie-In Agreements) are unlawful. (This is a seller who requires a customer buying one product also to buy a second product in order to get the first product.)

18.7   THE FTC AND CONSUMER PROTECTION

The **Federal Trade Commission (FTC)** has some authority over business in the field of *Consumer Protection.*

The Federal Trade Commission was set up by the Federal Trade Commission Act of 1914, and the Commission was to regulate trade, but had little power.

The Warranty-Federal Trade Commission Improvement Act of 1975 gave the Commission power to prescribe enforceable rules for the first time. The FTC has now issued rules on advertising eyeglasses, funeral industry advertising, vocational advertising, and children's advertising.

The Federal Trade Commission Improvement Act of 1980 limited the FTC's rule-making authority and made it more accountable to Congress.

FTC investigates *Unfair Business Practices.* It first tries to get the firm to change its practices voluntarily with a *Consent Order.* If this is not enough, it later issues a *Formal Complaint.* If this fails, the case is taken before an *Administrative Law Judge.* The case may be appealed to Federal Court.

The FTC also issues *Advisory Opinions* regarding the legality of a firm's proposed activities.

The FTC issues *Rules for an Entire Industry.* So far, these are only *Proposed Rules* and not yet enforceable by law.

EXAMPLE

For instance, the FTC has proposed that the funeral industry publish its rates.

The FTC investigates *Unfair or Deceptive Trade Practices.* These are practices that *offend public policy, are immoral, unethical or unscrupulous, and cause material or substantial harm to the consumer.*

— The FTC investigates misleading labeling, misleading product names, disparagement of competition, and violations of warranties.

— Now the FTC will investigate misleading advertising if it contains a *Material* (important) *Misrepresentation or omission that would likely mislead a consumer acting reasonably under the circumstances.*

— Deceptive labeling is examined by the FTC. The product must contain the elements included in the label.

18.8 FAIR EMPLOYMENT PRACTICES

Laws setting up *Fair Employment Practices* for businesses add to government control of hiring practices.

The **Civil Rights Act of 1964** makes it unlawful for employers, unions, or employment agencies to make any decision concerning the employment or work status of an individual based on race, sex, religion, or national origin.

Executive Order 11246 prohibits contractors from discriminating against employees or applicants because of race, sex, religion, or national origin. It requires *Affirmative Action* by employers to assure that applicants are employed without regard to race, sex, religion, or national origin.

The **Equal Pay Act of 1963** prohibits unequal pay for equal work regardless of sex, at managerial levels in state and local government as well as most private industries.

The **National Labor Relations Act of 1935** prohibits employers from refusing to engage in collective bargaining with a union selected by its employees.

The **Age Discrimination in Employment Act of 1967** prohibits discrimination in employment based on the age of people.

The **Vocational Rehabilitation Act of 1973** prohibits discrimination against handicapped individuals by the federal government, by private employers having government contracts, and by those firms receiving federal government financial assistance.

Affirmative Action Programs are designed to carry out equal-opportunity laws.

— Employers must eliminate discriminatory tests, non-job-related employment requirements, and other standards that have discriminatory effects when applied.

— Employers must take further affirmative steps to increase female and minority group participation in their work forces. This obligation is a *Remedy* for the *Present Effects of Past Discrimination.* (If the firm does not initiate effective *Affirmative Action Plans* after a hearing before an Administrative Law Judge, the government can withdraw all federal funds.)

18.9 LABOR RELATIONS

Labor Relations have seen big changes over the years. Until the early 1930's, most government laws seemed to favor management over labor.

The Railway Labor Act of 1926 required the railroads and their employees to attempt to make employment agreements through representatives chosen by each side.

The **Norris-LaGuardia Act** of 1932 protected peaceful strikes, picketing, and boycotts. Courts could no longer issue injunctions against unions participating in peaceful strikes.

The **National Labor Relations Act** of 1935 allowed employees to engage in collective bargaining and to strike.

The **Labor Management Relations Act** (Taft-Hartley Act) of 1947 gave lists of forbidden activities for management and for labor. Employers were allowed to propagandize against unions prior to National Labor Relations Board elections in the plant. *Closed Shops* were made illegal. (*Closed Shops* require union membership *Prior to Employment.)*

The **Labor Management Reporting and Disclosure Act**

(Landrum-Griffin Act) of 1959 strictly regulates internal union business procedures. Union elections must be by secret ballot. Ex-convicts and Communists are forbidden from holding union office. Union officials are made accountable for union property and funds. Most Secondary Boycotts are made illegal. *(Secondary Boycotts* are where friends of strikers refuse to buy products made by the firm being struck. They are also refusal to buy products of firms not being struck. Some of these are now legal under recent law.) (See Chapter 9, Part 8 for a more detailed discussion.)

State Workers' Compensation Acts allow compensation for workers injured on the job without regard to the existence of negligence or fault.

The **Occupational Health and Safety Act** of 1970 insures safe and healthful working conditions for practically every employee in the country.

18.10 RETIREMENT AND SECURITY INCOME

Retirement and Security Income have been important since 1935 in the U.S. These laws have been designed to protect employees and their families by covering the financial impact of retirement, disability, death, hospitalization, and unemployment.

The **Social Security Act** of 1935 required both employers and employees to contribute to give employees pension payments in old age and to pay expenses to survivors of employees who have died.

Medicare is a health insurance program administered by the Social Security Administration for people 65 years of age and older and for some disabled people under age 65. The two parts are *Hospital Costs* and *Doctors' Fees.*

The **Employee Retirement Income Security Act** of 1974 regulates retirement plans set up by employers for their employees. If these private pension plans meet the act's requirements, employers may deduct contributions to the plans as business expenses when computing their income taxes.

The Federal Unemployment Tax Act created a state system that provides unemployment compensation to eligible individuals.

Child Labor Laws prohibit oppressive child labor. Children under 16 years of age cannot be employed full time except by a parent under certain circumstances; nor can children between the ages of 16 and 18 be employed in hazardous jobs or in jobs detrimental to their health and well-being. Most states require children under 16 years of age to obtain work permits.

The **Wage and Hour Act** of 1935 provided that employees working over 40 hours per week are paid time-and-one-half for overtime.

18.11 ACCOUNTANTS' & CORPORATE OFFICERS' LIABILITY

Accountants are Liable for their Standards of Conduct under the Securities Act of 1933 and under the Securities Exchange Act of 1934. They are also liable for Breach of Contract, Negligence, and Fraud. As professionals, accountants are also supposed to keep records according to Generally Accepted Accounting Principles and Generally Accepted Auditing Standards.

Breach of Contract is a chief type of liability for accountants. If they do not follow the terms of the contract between themselves and their clients, they must pay damages to the clients.

Accountants are Liable for Negligence. They hold themselves out as professionals and receive pay for their services. They are held to the *Care, Knowledge, and Judgment* generally possessed by accountants.

— Accountants must *Act in Good Faith* so they will not be held liable for negligence.

— Accountants are not usually held liable for *Incorrect Judgment.*

— Accountants are not usually held liable for discovering or not discovering every impropriety, defalcation, or fraud on the books.

Accountants are Liable for Fraud. Fraud is intentionally misstating an important fact to mislead the client. *Constructive Fraud* is when an accountant is grossly negligent in the performance of duties.

Accountants have Liability to Third Parties, because much of an accountant's work is preparing financial statements that will be read and studied by third parties.

— A Third Party may sue an accountant if the third party relied on the accountant's work and was misled thereby.

— A Third Party may also hold the accountant liable for actual or constructive fraud.

Accountants are sometimes liable under the Securities Act of 1933.

— When new issues of securities are made by a corporation, the corporation must file with the Securities and Exchange Commission a Registration Statement.

— If the accountant prepared and certified financial statements included in the Registration Statement, and there were misstatements and omissions of *Material Facts,* the accountant could be held liable to anyone who purchased a security covered by the registration statement. The accountant must prove that he or she *Exercised Due Diligence* in the preparation of the financial statements.

Accountants' Liability Under the Securities and Exchange Act of 1934 follows:

— The accountant's liability is not so great under the 1934 act as under the 1933 act.

— An accountant is still liable for any false or misleading statement that affected the price of the security.

— It must also be proven that the purchaser or seller of the security *Relied Upon* the false or misleading statement in making the stock purchase and was not aware of the inaccuracy of the statement.

Accountants can be found criminally liable under both the 1933 and 1934 ***Acts for Willful Conduct.***

In the wake of corporate and accounting scandals like those that affected Enron and WorldCom, both of which ended up in bankruptcy proceedings, the Sarbanes-Oxley Act of 2002 was signed into law by President George W. Bush on July 30, 2002. It mandates wide-ranging public company accounting and disclosure reforms. Highlighting the Act is a provision requiring CEOs and CFOs of some of the largest U.S. companies to certify the accuracy of their annual and quarterly reports. A violation of Rules of the Public Company Accounting Oversight Board is treated as a violation of, and gives rise to the same penalties as, the 1934 Act.

18.12 INTERNATIONAL LAW

International Law now affects many business dealings, because we have a *Global Economy.* Some *sources of International Law* are *Treaties,* the *Statute of the International Court of Justice, International Organizations* and *Conferences, and Resolutions of the United Nations.*

Transacting Business Abroad involves more risks because of distance, currency fluctuations, languages, and laws.

— Banks issue *Letters of Credit* for business transactions between U.S. and foreign businesses.

— Under a Letter of Credit the issuing bank is bound to pay the seller when the seller has complied with the terms and conditions of the Letter of Credit. The seller looks to the issuing bank, not to the buyer, when it presents the documents required by the Letter of Credit.

— Often the Letter of Credit will require the seller to deliver a *Bill of Lading* to prove that the shipment has been made.

— **Letters of Credit** assure sellers of payment while at the same time they assure the buyer that payment will not be made until the sellers have complied with the terms and conditions of the credit.

Foreign Sales Contracts should be in writing. A clause should mention which language should officially be used in interpreting the contract.

— The **Contract of Sale** should include a legal definition of terms, *The Price and Manner of Payment,* and the *Acceptable Currency for Payment.*

— A **Choice-Of-Law Clause** in the contract states which law shall be used in the event of a dispute or breach of contract.

— A clause should be included in the contract protecting the parties from *Forces Beyond Their Control.*

— An **Arbitration Clause** could be included in the contract.

Methods of settling differences between businesspeople of two different countries having different laws are:

1. **Act of State Doctrine** is a legal doctrine stating that the court of the first country will not examine the validity of public acts committed by a recognized second country within the territory of the second country. If it did so, it would vex the harmony of the international relations between the two countries.

2. **The Principle of Comity** also comes into effect when the law of one nation is different from international law. This Principle of Comity is the deference by which one nation gives effect to the laws and judicial decrees of another nation, based primarily on *Respect.*

Sovereign Immunity immunizes foreign nations from the jurisdiction of the U.S. after certain conditions are satisfied. The Foreign Sovereign Immunities Act of 1976 modified this doctrine.

— This law determines the circumstances in which a legal action can be brought against a foreign nation in the United States.

— Federal courts, rather than the Department of State, now determine claims of foreign sovereign immunity.

— A foreign nation is not immune from the jurisdiction of the

U.S. courts when the action is *based upon a commercial activity carried on in the United States by a foreign nation.*

Foreign persons and foreign governments may sue under U.S. antitrust laws in U.S. courts, if the alleged violation had a substantial effect on U.S. commerce.

Common Markets are two or more countries organizing and integrating their economies into cohesive groups.

The **European Economic Community** currently includes 12 Western European nations, lifting tariffs and restrictive agreements among themselves. Also, common tariffs are in force between European Economic Community nations and other nations.

The Treaty of Rome in 1957 not only set up the European Economic Community, it also provided a promotion of free movement of workers, goods, and capital among the member nations.

Other Common Markets are: Central American Common Market, the Caribbean Community, the Common Market of French-Speaking African States, and the Council for Mutual Economic Assistance of the Communist States.

The agreement between the United States and Canada gradually cutting down trade barriers between the two countries should result eventually in a North American Common Market.

REVIEW QUESTIONS

1. What is Product Liability?
The price a product manufacturer will have to pay for fail-

ing to exercise reasonable care in the manufacture of items that may cause physical harm to the users of the product.

2. What can a product manufacturer do to help cut down potential liability?

Test and inspect the products before selling them, and place warning statements on the products including dangers of misuse.

3. Why was the Electronic Fund Transfer Act of 1978 passed?

To protect consumers and businesses using automatic machines to transfer funds.

4. How long does a customer using electronic machines have to complain?

Sixty days after receiving the statement from the financial institution.

5. After receiving a customer complaint, how long does the financial institution have to investigate and report back to the customer?

Ten days.

6. After a customer's card is lost or stolen, how long does the customer have to report this fact to the financial institution without incurring great loss?

Two days.

7. If the customer reports loss of card within two days, what is the maximum loss the customer is subject to?

The lesser of $50 or the amount of the transfer.

8. What is Collateral?

Property put up by the debtor to be given or kept by the creditor in case of default; or merchandise in the warehouse of the buyer that has not yet been paid for and therefore can be claimed by the seller if there is a security agreement backed up by a financing statement filed at the courthouse or some other appropriate government office.

9. Why should a Security Agreement be filed with the proper governmental authority?

To protect the creditor. In case the buyer defaults, and two or more creditors claim the same property, the creditor who filed the financing statement first will win out.

10. Is Bankruptcy a state law or a federal law?

Federal.

11. What is the purpose of a person or business filing for bankruptcy?

Protection against suits by creditors.

12. How does bankruptcy benefit creditors?

It distributes the debtor's assets among the creditors in a fair way.

13. How does bankruptcy benefit debtors?

It gives them a new financial start.

14. How does Voluntary Bankruptcy differ from Involuntary Bankruptcy?

In Voluntary Bankruptcy, the debtor begins legal proceedings, while in Involuntary Bankruptcy, the creditor begins legal proceedings.

15. When a person goes into bankruptcy, does the person lose all his or her assets?

No, the bankrupt can keep some value in the home, car, household furnishings, clothing, appliances, musical instruments, animals, and personal crops, some jewelry, tools of trade, life insurance, social security, and unemployment compensation.

16. In what order are a bankrupt's debts paid?

Secured creditors are paid first, then bankruptcy administration fees are paid next, then business and financial debts, then employee wages and salaries and commissions, then payments owed to employee retirement funds, then customer deposits, then government tax claims, and finally general claims.

17. What is meant by the term Discharge of Debts?

The judge clears the bankrupt from the legal liability of paying the remainder of the debts that the bankrupt owes.

18. How does Chapter 11 Bankruptcy differ from Chapter 7 Bankruptcy?

In Chapter 7 Bankruptcy, the Trustee sells most of the bankrupt's assets to pay creditors' claims. In Chapter 11 Bankruptcy, the business is allowed to continue to operate under the guidance of a trustee or a Creditors' Committee.

19. Why is a Plan of Organization often set up in a Chapter 11 Bankruptcy?

It is a plan of payment of debts. If this plan is approved by the court, it must be followed by the debtor and the creditors alike. It often allows creditors eventually to be paid in full.

20. Why does the Securities and Exchange Commission require that corporations issuing new securities register them with the Securities and Exchange Commission and issue complete prospectuses?

So that the Securities and Exchange Commission can have some control over new corporate stock and bond issues, and so that prospective investors can know exactly what they are buying.

21. What is a Prospectus?

A detailed information sheet, published by the corporation, giving information about the corporation and the new issue which they are trying to sell, such as stocks or bonds.

22. What is a Proxy?

A written form which a stockholder may use to vote on questions coming up at the stockholders' meeting. The stockholder signs this form, mailing it to corporate headquarters, giving other persons the power to vote on these questions for the stockholder in case of absence.

23. How does the Securities and Exchange Commission have some control regarding unfriendly corporate take-overs?

Through the Williams Act which requires any person or group buying or acquiring more than 5% of a class of securities to file a statement with the Securities and Exchange Commission giving details as to their plans and purposes in acquiring the stock.

24. In a hostile takeover attempt of one corporation by another, which corporation must file with the Securities and Exchange Commission?

Both corporations.

25. What is a boycott?

A refusal to buy the products of a certain company.

26. Are boycotts illegal?

Secondary boycotts are illegal but primary boycotts are legal.

27. How does a Primary Boycott differ from a Secondary Boycott?

Primary boycotts are when strikers refuse to buy the products produced by the corporation against whom they are striking. A Secondary Boycott is where strikers persuade other unions and other groups to refuse to buy these products.

28. What is a Tie-In Agreement?

If you want to buy one product, you must also buy a second product.

29. Are Tie-In Agreements legal?

No.

30. What is one of the chief goals of the Federal Trade Commission?

To prevent deceptive advertising.

31. What is Affirmative Action?

A law requiring employers to increase female and minority group participation in the work force.

32. How does the government force affirmative action on employers?

By threatening to withdraw federal funds.

33. How does a Closed Shop differ from a Union Shop?

In a Closed Shop, a prospective employee must join the union before being hired on the job. In a Union Shop, the employer may hire anyone that the employer desires, but after being hired, the employee must join the union.

34. What is the Employee Retirement Income Security Act of 1974?

It gives guidelines to employers who wish to set up retirement plans for their employees.

35. What happens if the retirement plans are approved by the government?

Employers may deduct contributions to these plans as business expenses when computing their income taxes.

36. Are accountants usually held liable for incorrect judgment?

No.

37. If the United States is a sovereign nation, are we forced to abide by International Law?

No.

38. In what ways does the United States cooperate with International Law even though it is a sovereign nation?

We make treaties with other nations, we are part of the United Nations, we attend International Conferences, and we take part in the International Court.

39. What are the three parties to a Letter of Credit?

Buyer, Seller, and Bank.